VIBRANT FAITH IN THE CONGREGATION

In Memory of
James Francis (Jim) Mullen
1957–2011

VIBRANT FAITH
IN THE
CONGREGATION

David W. Anderson

Vibrant Faith Publishing
is a service of
Vibrant Faith Ministries

Publishing Consultant: Huff Publishing Associates, LLC
Cover images © iStockphoto. Used by permission.
Cover and book design: Jessica Hillstrom, Hillspring Books

Library of Congress Cataloging-in-Publication Data

ISBN 978-1-889407-51-7

Manufactured in the U.S.A.

14 13 12 11 10 09 1 2 3 4 5 6 7 8 9 10

CONTENTS

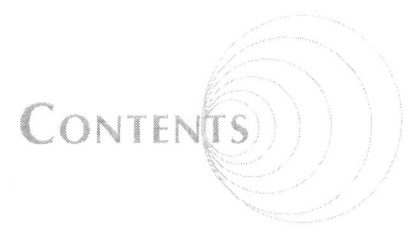

SERIES FOREWORD

Being a Christian in North America early in the twenty-first century is probably more like being a first-century Christian than being a Christian in the 1950s. Granted, American Christians are not being fed to lions, or used as tiki torches (yes, Nero did that!) to light the royal courtyard in Rome. Nonetheless, with Christianity in sharp decline in the United States, compared with the 1950s Christians are increasingly in the minority. Even if they are not being actively persecuted, they are losing power.

Robert Putnam and David Campbell's excellent book, *American Grace,* clearly documents a huge shift in American Christian religiosity. Whereas the 1950s were the Golden Era of American religious involvement, and the '60s the decade of secularism, the '80s saw the rise of Christian evangelicalism in the '80s, and now at the beginning of the twenty-first century Americans (especially the young) are basically saying, "I'll have none of it!"

Christianity no longer plays the dominant role in shaping the American religious and cultural landscape that it did in the 1950s. Rather, Christianity is one voice among many vying for the hearts, minds, and values of the American populace.

The Apostle Paul in the first century faced a similar context. Acts 17:16 and following tells of Paul entering the Areopagus in Athens, a place of debate and discussion where a wide spectrum of religious and philosophical perspectives were tossed around. Paul spoke there saying, "Athenians, I see how extremely religious you are in every way. For as I went through the city and looked carefully at the objects of your worship, I found among them an altar with the inscription, 'To an unknown god'. What therefore you worship as unknown, this I proclaim to you." (vs. 22-23, NRSV). Paul then goes on to speak of God's revelation through Jesus Christ, noting that in him "we live and have our being" (vs. 28). Christianity in Paul's time was, to use today's market language, a "start-up" in a very competitive religious marketplace. For those early Christians it wasn't easy because Christianity was not the "big dog" religion.

If Christianity in America in the 1950s was the "big dog," by the 1990s and to the present, other "start ups" and older, competing religious and philosophical voices have displaced what used to be. For all practical purposes, like Paul, Christians are back in the Areopagus debating the merits of the Christian faith amidst many competing religious voices.

Persevering in their faith was hard for first-century Christian leaders and it is getting harder for twenty-first-century Christian leaders. Low morale now often permeates the ranks of pastors, Christian educators, musicians, youth workers, and judicatory leaders. Attendance is down, budgets are down, and congregations are aging and not being replaced by new younger people.

In other words, it's a perfect time to be a Christian leader in America! Christianity has always been most effective when not tethered to the cultural trappings of the larger society. As a lay movement committed to transforming lives through faith in Jesus Christ, Christianity has, historically, been able to thrive and make a difference. By not being tethered to the culture or the recent past Christian leaders can innovate, adapt, reclaim, and reframe the best of our faith and its traditions.

At Vibrant Faith Ministries, we embrace these times and work to be nimble, adaptive, and creative, while grounded in the enduring love of God through Jesus Christ. To us, this is what the times call for and what vibrant faith enables us to do.

This second book in the series written by my colleague and friend, Dr. David Anderson, demonstrates how Christian leaders can adapt, innovate, and find new life in their ministries. Dr. Anderson is writing from the world of experience. Examples of innovation, stories of transformation, and illustrations of game-changing ministry dominate this book. He is drawing from his many years of coaching congregational leaders. His narrative is really their narrative. And those leaders are telling him about real transformation and innovation, not just theory. His writing tells of the best practices he has found.

My suggestion to the reader is the following:

1. Get over it: the 1950s are gone. We are living in the era of the Areopagus, a marketplace of ideas and discussion.

2. It's going to be difficult to do ministry during these times. (When hasn't it been so?)

3. It's the perfect time for Christians to innovate, adapt, and experiment in ministry.

4. The Vibrant Faith Frame that shapes the ideas Dr. Anderson presents here is an excellent way of engaging these times in transformational ways.

And most significantly,

5. Jesus is Lord in all centuries and in all places. So let us take heart that God goes with us, providing courage and energy for each new day.

Paul Hill
Executive Director
Vibrant Faith Ministries

INTRODUCTION

Vibrant Faith in the Congregation is the second book in the three-part Vibrant Faith: Home and Congregation Series. The first book, *From the Great Omission to Vibrant Faith:The Role of the Home in Renewing the Church*, identifies the critical role of the home in Christian faith formation, a role that has often been overlooked in the life of the contemporary church in America. The book begins with a study of the Great Omission (the ignored role of the home) that includes modern culture, faith formation research, biblical analysis, and then a description of the Vibrant Faith Frame that can be an antidote to the Great Omission. The remainder of the book attends to the role of congregational leadership and how that leadership can respond to the Great Omission in a way that helps promote the Great Commission (Matthew 28:19-20) to make disciples of all nations. It presents concrete and practical strategies for effective ways to lead the congregation into the Vibrant Faith Frame.

Vibrant Faith in the Congregation offers congregational leaders practical ways to apply the Vibrant Faith Frame to various ministries of the congregation. More specifically, this second book in the trilogy focuses on concrete ways the Vibrant Faith Frame assists congregations in facing up to the Great Omission in order to more fully accomplish the task given by Jesus in the Great Commission. An underlying theme of the book addresses the important task for the church to be missional, that is, to help people live out the gospel in word and deed in homes, congregation, community, and the larger world.

The role of the church in the life of individuals, households, and larger society is waning. Our time has been described as post-Christian, an era when the church and Christianity no longer shape people's schedules, daily lives, and values. Wednesdays are no longer recognized in most local communities and schools as "church night." Even Sunday mornings are seldom sacrosanct moments protected from the competition of sports events. Fewer people attend church; fewer people associate themselves with specific denominations and congregations. The number of non-Christian adherents continues to grow. At the same time, the United States population continues to think and talk about God at a rate that appears to be higher than most countries, but whether or not that theological discourse and the related values and creeds expressed by Americans are actually Christian is doubtful. Recent research indicates that the dominant religious value in America is best described as "moralistic, therapeutic deism," a religious conviction of staying out of trouble, being happy and successful, and using any god to get one there. It is a religion that appears to have taken over historic and biblical Christianity.

It might be tempting to blame the larger society for getting it all wrong, but the more engaging response would be to recognize what the church can do to more effectively address people's lives with a living hope in Christ. This book is dedicated to that kind of response, one that promotes a grassroots outreach partnering local congregations with homes that are equipped to bring God's healing, renewing, and creative powers to hurting lives and times.

The distinctions between civil religion present in our time and biblical Christianity have always existed. One only needs to look at Luke 4:16-30 for a biblical example of this. In no uncertain terms Jesus announces that his life is the fulfillment of the prophetic message in Isaiah. At first the people hear this home-town boy with delight, but then when he confronts the people of Nazareth with their embedded religious and political chauvinism, they want to kill him right on the spot. Likewise, the challenge for the church has always been to preach, teach, and serve in a way that is faithful to the gospel and empowered by the Spirit of Christ to redeem lives, without glossing over hatred, prejudices, nationalism, or other false teachings.

The primary purpose of the book and the larger trilogy is to attend to how the teaching, preaching, and all other efforts to transmit the gospel by the grace of God can actually be received, believed, and lived. Congregations present the gospel in word and deed through a variety of ministries. This book will explore such ministry topics as evangelism, Christian education, worship and preaching, youth and family, stewardship, administration, preschool and after school programs, and congregational facility design.

The chapters associated with each of these topics do not pretend to say everything there is to say about these ministry agendas. The chapters simply identify and embellish how the Vibrant Faith Frame impacts those areas of ministry to advance the missional outreach of the church in a post-Christian era. More could be written about each of these important topics, but what is written will greatly assist and enhance the work of congregational leaders committed to the Vibrant Faith Frame.

The Vibrant Faith Frame

To maximize the benefits of this book, the reader will need to keep in mind the Vibrant Faith Frame, language, and concepts that will be referenced throughout the book. What follows is a review of that language described in detail in chapter two of *From the Great Omission to Vibrant Faith*. A brief description of the Vibrant Faith Frame with its essential language is presented here for the reader's convenience. The *Appendix* contains the Vibrant Faith Frame language without description for easy reference while reading the following chapters.

Six Locations of Ministry: God's Activity in All the World

The Six Locations of Ministry identify the focus of the church's activity in the world. That activity is personal and local as well as universal. The Six Locations of Ministry acknowledge that the work of the people of God is everywhere. The Vibrant Faith Frame emphasizes a strategic focus on children and youth. Research has shown that if the church does not have meaningful contact with people by the time they are in their early teens, it is quite unlikely that they will ever claim Jesus Christ as Savior and Lord. At the same time, to care for people and their journey of faith is also to care about their everyday needs for food, shelter, and warmth. This represents the Christian faith and life reflected in the Bible (see Isaiah 58:6-11; Micah 6:8; Matthew 25:31-46; 1 Timothy 5:8; James 1:27). The care the body of Christ places on one's neighbor has no limits. To care for people as an act of faith in the saving work of Jesus Christ means engaging with and caring for home, community, and creation itself. The Six Locations of Ministry name the contexts that our incarnational God—the God disclosed in Jesus who enters the world as fully embodied and unconditionally part of creation—expects us to enter with grace, mercy, and peace. Those arenas of care the Vibrant Faith Frame identifies as:

1. Children and Youth
2. Homes
3. Congregations
4. Community
5. Culture
6. Creation

The Five Principles: Elements of a Vibrant Church

The Five Principles identify the relational nature of the church. This foundational orientation helps congregational leaders see the work of the church beyond the venue of congregational activities. Through a variety of relationships and daily life experiences the Holy Spirit works in people's lives to form faith. The church that lives as the community of saints includes—but involves more than—a weekly experience in a local congregation. The life and work of the church incorporates the primary life setting of our daily lives (referenced here as "home") with the more public setting of faith communities in congregations. Broadening the understanding of church and how faith is formed has deep implications for most every aspect of a congregation's life and its leadership. The Five Principles that follow help congregational leaders keep their attention on this vital and more encompassing understanding of church, the body of Christ:

1. Faith is formed by the power of the Holy Spirit through personal, trusted relationships—often in our own homes.
2. The church is a living partnership between the ministry of the congregation and the ministry of the home.
3. Where Christ is present in faith, the home is church, too.
4. Faith is caught more than it is taught.
5. If we want Christian children and youth, we need Christian adults/parents.

The Four Keys: Faith Practices for Living One's Baptism

The common thread that gives life to the following chapters is the Four Keys. These keys articulate a foundational spirituality that shapes the work of congregations and the lives of Christians. Faith is formed through relationships, and those relationships engage in fundamental Christian practices. These basic faith practices are evident in Scripture, church history, and modern research. It is through such practices that faith is transmitted between the generations and over time. They take place during Sunday worship services as well as at a dinner table at home. The Four Keys present a way of life that is simple, doable, replicable, and helpful for all congregational ministries as well as all disciples of Christ in their daily lives. Those Four Key practices are:

1. Caring Conversation
2. Devotions
3. Service
4. Rituals and Traditions

AAA Christian Disciples: What a Follower of Jesus Looks Like

The goal of congregational ministry is to make disciples of Jesus. Christian disciples are not perfect saints, just forgiven sinners, people who are real, not pretend. One could call them authentic. A disciple of Christ is called to enter into the world that God loves in order to heal, reconcile, and serve in Christ's name. That means Christians can't hide away. They are to be in the world, available and serving. Their service and their witness is on behalf of the Triune God who has already won the great battle of life and death, good and evil. The Christian lives affirming God's goodness and victory in Christ. The Christian also lives affirming that God is alive and well blessing, serving, and gifting lives to do the work of the reign of God on earth today. Hence, a way to describe Christians is to say they are AAA:

1. Authentic
2. Available
3. Affirming

Who the Book Is For

Vibrant Faith in the Congregation is intended for congregational leaders, be they staff, elected, volunteer, or appointed servants of the congregation. It is also for those who work with and train those same congregational leaders. Certain members of the various ministry teams will want to focus on the chapter or chapters that relate directly to their own work in the congregation, and that is fine. But it is also important and helpful for people in the various ministry teams—and especially staff and governing boards—to read and reflect on the other chapters. Because the ministry of the congregation is truly one ministry, it is important that people working on a particular area consider how their work impacts others and how other ministry areas can be of service to one's own areas of responsibility.

For good worship and good preaching enhance youth and family ministry; youth and family ministry includes Christian education; Christian education serves as a form of evangelism—and so on. It is important to recognize what holds these various areas of ministry together as one ministry so that various leaders and strategies do not end up living in their own little worlds, disconnected from the larger whole of the life of the congregation. The Vibrant Faith Frame understands the various ministries as serving a greater whole, and that greater whole is presented over and over again in the various chapters.

The third book of the trilogy, *Vibrant Faith in the Home,* also reinforces the unity of the ministry of the church. It will explore the critical dynamic of living the gospel of Jesus Christ in word and deed in daily lives. The home is more than an address where one resides. It represents the primary life setting in which the Christian life and faith can blossom and bless the larger world for the sake of the cross of Christ. Just as evangelism and Christian education take place in and through the life of a congregation and weave together as part of a larger whole, so does the work of Christians serving in the congregation weave together with the work of those same Christians serving in and through the home. The more Christian ministry is seen as a whole—the vision behind the Vibrant Faith Frame—the more effective the church will be in all aspects of its life, especially as it seeks to reach out to the larger world with the grace, mercy, and peace of God in Christ.

EVANGELISM:
BEING CHURCH IN CONGREGATION, HOMES, AND COMMUNITY

The Mayor of Bergen, Norway invited me to his home to enjoy a Sunday afternoon meal and conversation with his family and other guests. After the meal he took out his Bible and read a passage that had been used in his congregation that morning. He read it slowly, reflected on a point in the text that was important to him, and then opened up the conversation to others. It began a flow of thoughts from many of us present. The conversations conveyed a sense of wonderment and awe at the power of God's word for our lives and world. The conversations were not didactic or dogmatic, simply reflective, open, and gentle. I left his home that day knowing I had experienced the good news of Jesus Christ and the community of saints.

The activity of the mayor gathered with family and guests represents the larger understanding of evangelism endorsed by the Vibrant Faith Frame—that evangelism is a way of life that reflects the love of God in Christ wherever a Christian lives and breathes.

Yet instead many see evangelism as a subset of activities in the life of a congregation or larger church body. Those few attending to the evangelism of a congregation (often those on an "evangelism committee" or serving on staff with responsibilities for evangelism) dedicate their work to growing the life of the congregation, often with specific goals of growing the congregation numerically, by bringing new people into the faith community. Evangelism, therefore, becomes the work of outreach into the community to bring people into the life of the congregation. It also has implications for attending to new visitors and to visitors who continue to worship in the congregation over time, incorporating new members into the life of the congregation, and promoting ways to make the ministry of the congregation more visible to the surrounding community, known as good advertising or marketing. All of this is to add to the membership rolls to strengthen the witness of the Christian faith into homes, neighborhoods, communities, and, finally, into all the world.

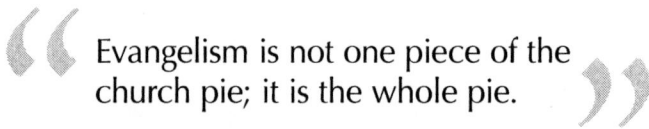

> Evangelism is not one piece of the church pie; it is the whole pie.

This orientation to evangelism is heavy on the assignment of a few and involves programmatic or administrative steps to fulfill the work of evangelism. It assumes that being a bearer of good news is a delegated task rather than a way of life common to all disciples. That orientation stands in tension with the commitment of the Vibrant Faith Frame that understands faith as formed by God through relationships, not programs; friends, family, and even strangers, not primarily "experts" (i.e., congregational leadership); and daily life experiences, not committees. Of course, it is not an either/or—either relationships or programs, experts, and committees. The Vibrant Faith Frame emphasizes the role of relationships through the whole evangelical quest and knows evangelism as a way of life that is authentic, available, and affirming of God's work and will on behalf of all that God creates. In the Vibrant Faith Frame, evangelism is not one piece of the church pie; it is the whole pie. The Vibrant Faith Frame implicitly suggests an understanding of and strategies for the evangelism of the church. This chapter emphasizes the Vibrant Faith Frame's attention to the ministry of a congregation in partnership with the ministry of the home. That vital partnership promotes an approach to evangelism that simply cannot be contained within the typical efforts of an evangelism committee that seeks to draw in visitors and new members. Specifically, this chapter focuses on evangelism through 1) ministry to the larger community served by the congregation, 2) Christian hospitality and outreach through homes, and, 3) Milestones Ministry. All of these contributions have the common denominator of developing faith-forming relationships within and between various generations.

The Vibrant Faith Frame Perspective on Evangelism

Evangelism represents Jesus' culminating message and directive to his disciples in Matthew 28:19 to "Go," a directive for the people of the evangel (meaning "good news"). The Greek for "Go" can and should be translated "As you are going" which fits quite well with the understanding of evangelism presented here. As we are working, playing, living, and worshipping, we live out this command from Jesus by letting our lives in congregations, in our households, and everyplace else we "are going" teach others in word and deed about God's good news in Christ.

This passage in Matthew 28 comes at the very end of the Gospel of Matthew. The beginning of The Acts of the Apostles conveys a similar message. Now that everything that needed to happen has occurred, the apostles are being sent out "to the ends of the earth" (1:8). The narrative of the life, death, and resurrection of Jesus is the hope of the world that needs to reach everyone, not just an inner circle of beneficiaries. " . . . [B]aptizing . . . and teaching them to obey everything I have commanded you" (Matthew 28:20) commends a way of life that is incumbent on all, not just for the attention of a few. It marks *the* way to live in this present age. Jesus sends out the disciples not with a disembodied message to consider or reject but as an embodied community living out the good news in ways that make it plain to the culture. The Four Key faith practices offer a simple and succinct way to embody God's reign in the world each day and in all settings. The good news shapes the conversations they have, the message to which they are devoted, the passion to serve others, and the nonverbal and verbal cues that suggest through rituals and traditions the values and priorities of God's reign.

> "As you are going," enter into God's world with God's reign of grace, mercy, and peace in Christ.

The work of evangelism sends people out into God's world with something that deserves the broadest audience possible, something identified in the Vibrant Faith Frame through the Six Locations of Ministry. Jesus does not reduce the message of "Come to me, all you that are weary and are carrying heavy burdens, and I will give you rest" (Matthew 11:28) to mean he'll give us a weekly respite in a Sunday morning pew. The same Jesus who says, "Come to me" also says, "As you are going," enter into God's world with God's reign of grace, mercy, and peace in Christ. (See Luke 10:1-12 for a preliminary run through of this approach to evangelism, this approach to living with good news). Jesus' whole life and message communicate this. Read the Six Locations of Ministry of the Vibrant Faith Frame through the eyes of evangelism this way:

- *Individual lives, especially children and youth*: Wherever you are, welcome children and all other "little ones" as God's beloved ones.
- *Homes:*Approach others, eat with them at a table in homes and in the community, join others along the road and at other outdoor places in God's wondrous creation.

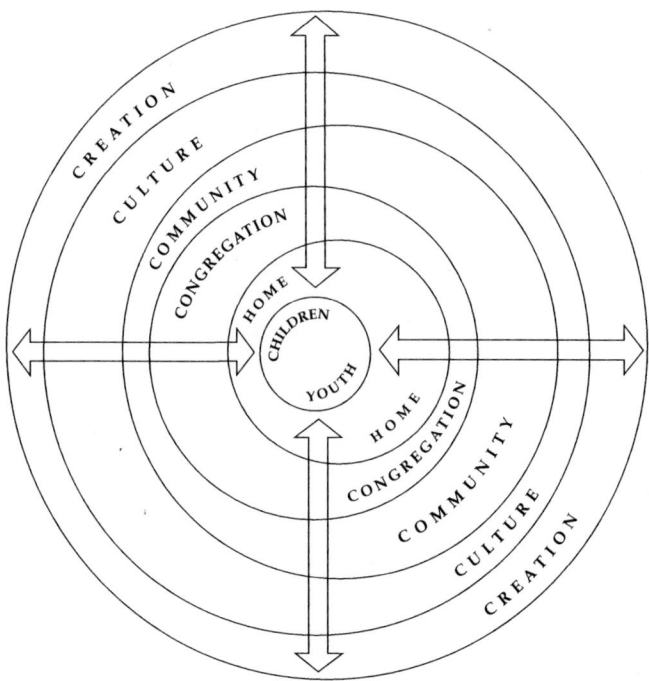

- *Congregation*: Worship, converse, and serve with others as God's holy people in homes, congregations, and other places too.
- *Community*: Live in community with others openly and lovingly with the gospel, teaching, healing, admonishing, encouraging, and renewing people along the way, not waiting for people to walk through congregational church doors; care for widows and orphans.
- *Culture*: Enter the larger culture, challenging religious and tribal stereotypes. Speak to and on behalf of the poor and others often forgotten in one's quest for success. Engage and question the religious, the economically, socially, and politically powerful and privileged, as well as the economic and social standards of the day; be stewards of the mysteries of God, not of culturally promoted prejudices.

- *Creation*: Honor and tend to God's creation as the place for all God's creatures to dwell by acknowledging the message revealed in the lives of the birds of the air and flowers of the fields and the praise of God in thunder, mountains, mighty cedars, oceans, fields, and more.

Christians are people of faith who live with and into the good news of life and salvation in Christ. They go out into all the corners of the world (the Six Locations of Ministry) with an understanding of and foundational strategies for the Christian community (the Five Principles that focus on outreach through relationships). Christians live into the Christian faith by practicing the faith (the Four Keys), and daily God resurrects disciples of Christ who are Authentic, Available, and Affirming (AAA Disciples).

Members of a congregation's evangelism committee might rush to this chapter and think, "What is in here for me?" when in fact there is something about evangelism in the other chapters as well. For the Vibrant Faith Frame is in itself a missional frame, and the mission of the body of Christ is to forgive, reconcile, heal, tend, break bread, speak, pray, teach, serve, love, praise, and live 24/7 as though the cross of Christ has already won the day, everyday forever. This is not a church growth frame, a seekers' frame, an evangelistic movement frame, or a proselytizing frame.[1] It is a frame that identifies the people of God as living with meaning and purpose derived from the reign of God in Christ, a reign that guides our own thoughts and actions as individuals and communities in Christ. Worship and preaching sends people out into the world with the gospel of Christ as the centerpiece of life itself. Christian education for faith formation teaches, preaches, and embodies a life that connects with God and others—all others—with the gospel. Youth and family ministry necessarily networks with a whole host of people, households, extended family and friends, neighborhoods, and people once known as strangers, binding them into a gospel community that serves the whole-life needs—including faith and spirituality—of children, youth, and adults. The list could go on to all the other chapters and areas of congregational life. All of them represent the evangelism of the church.

> The mission of the body of Christ is to forgive, reconcile, heal, tend, break bread, speak, pray, teach, serve, love, praise, and live 24/7 as though the cross of Christ has already won the day, everyday forever.

At the same time, this chapter does note three particular strategies based on the Vibrant Faith Frame: congregations serve the immediate community and not simply the members of a congregation; homes serve as outposts for the witness of the church to the larger community through the practice of Christian hospitality; and Milestones Ministry (see pp. 37-44 for details) provides a valuable link between people's daily life experiences and the Christian faith. We turn first to serving the immediate community.

Evangelism for the Local Community

The congregation of the recent past has had a proclivity to turn inward. Even its evangelism is dedicated to bringing people in rather than sending people out with the good news. This orientation to evangelism reflects an "attractional model" (bringing people in) instead of a missional model. Leaders focus on how to get people "more involved," usually meaning more regular in the worship life and activities of the congregation. Fortunately, more recently there has been a movement to concentrate on discipleship and not membership. The Vibrant Faith Frame supports that move.

Another way of stating this change of course for the life and purpose of congregations is the move from a focus on membership to serving the people living in the local area of the congregation, hence, the historic concept of *parish church*. The word parish connotes a geographic region that the local community of faith serves, that is, the people and environment near the congregation. It is time to reclaim the idea that the local congregation serves not only members but everyone in the local community within reach of the congregation's ministry.

This is not to limit the reach of a congregation away from global issues and relationships. It does endorse a ministry that does not jump from congregational members to overseas mission work. Sometimes it seems more exciting and exotic to do ministry half way around the world than in one's own backyard. Christian ministry is not an either/or. It is both/and, both an interest in global needs and an interest in local neighborhood needs for God's grace. In this, evangelism is countercultural. It aspires to be a way of life that reflects the life of the kingdom of God in Christ in any locale and in any context.

For some this shift of focus from serving members to serving the immediate community is a huge leap. For others it represents the very heart of the gospel. Indeed, this challenge of being the church for the world is not new. It was the challenge that Dietrich Bonhoeffer in the war-torn world of Germany stated in a letter from prison: "The church is the church only when it exists for others."[2] That conviction lies at the heart of evangelism. That conviction suggests a life that reaches out to individuals and homes, in and through congregations to communities, cultures, and creation. The parish church, the congregation that serves the immediate community, offers an image that takes the congregation beyond itself to the neighborhood and larger world of need with good news. The evangelism of the church, the entire body of Christ around the world, promotes and establishes personal contact, personal relationships with others wherever the people of God may be. That outreach takes place fundamentally through the sacrifice of giving one's time, commitment, and resources to attend to others, whether those others are in the next room, next door, in a shelter or business office downtown, or across the oceans on a college campus or in a refugee camp.

The Six Locations of Ministry that move from individuals, to homes, to congregation, and on to communities present an opportunity often missed by congregations: working with other congregations in the same locale, whether or not those other congregations embody the same or a similar heritage to one's own. It is time to recognize that various Christian traditions working together have much to offer the local community in both service and witness on behalf of Christ. The church is more authentic in the eyes of the young when it presents a common face to the world. That unity can be expressed through all the Four Keys of engaging as well as caring conversations, a common devotion to God's word, service in the name of Christ, and Christian rituals and traditions that Christians have in common as well as those that can arouse new imagination about the kingdom of God here and now. To be one in Christ, Christians don't have to speak the exact same language or use the same symbols and gestures. To say, "Jesus is Lord" (1 Corinthians 12:3) is to acknowledge that the Spirit of Christ has gifted everyone. This, too, is part of the evangelical witness to the world and evangelical outreach on behalf of a world filled with tears, misgivings, and fears, a world in need of the crucified and risen Christ.

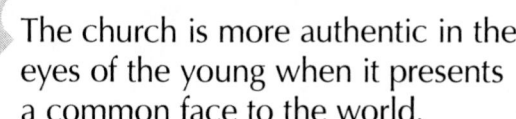

The church is more authentic in the eyes of the young when it presents a common face to the world.

The Evangelism of Christian Hospitality

The second way that the Vibrant Faith Frame impacts evangelism is through Christian hospitality. The front door of the ministry of the church is not located in a congregation's building that brings people in. The front door of the ministry of the church is located in all homes connected with the ministry of the church, the doors that lead people out into God's world with faith, hope, and love in Christ. Those doors of dwelling places that people enter in order to rest and reenergize and that they leave to serve, play, and praise are the doors to the evangelism of the church, the work of being people of the gospel in all settings of life.

Christian hospitality embodies the church that practices the Four Keys in and through the home. A grandparent personifies this who listens attentively on the phone to a teen's struggles at school and offers a word of encouragement and prayer with the promise to stay connected and pray regularly for the grandchild. That same grandparent can write a note via email or on paper to send thoughts of care and concern, and then, when they are together again, give a welcoming hug that reinforces the prior contact between the two. All of this exemplifies the evangelism of hospitality.

The doors of homes that welcome people in as well as send people out links evangelism to Christian hospitality, that way of life that is receptive to God and to those God gives into our care. It is no better expressed than in the words of the Apostle Paul, "Welcome one another, therefore, just as Christ has welcomed you, for the glory of God" (Romans 15:7). Christian hospitality as an image for evangelism often goes unnoticed and undervalued.

Such hospitality and such evangelism is not meant to be directed merely toward those who do not yet claim Jesus as Savior and Lord or the "once-churched" or the "inactives." Evangelism is for all, including those who are actively part of a congregation and gladly confess the name of Jesus Christ. Because all our lives experience the brokenness of human existence, Christians never fully acknowledge or embrace the gift of faith from God. Christians in worship routinely confess the sin of their human frailty and failure. The father's confession before Jesus—"I believe; help my unbelief!" (Mark 9:24b)— expresses the struggles not just of one man but of all who wish to follow Jesus. It is with good reason that the Apostle Paul addresses the church in Rome with the admonition to "Welcome one another as Christ has welcomed you for the glory of God." We all need that welcoming, inviting attitude that encourages and supports us on the journey of the Christian life and faith.

Hospitable Congregations

Congregations, of course, also serve as significant places for Christian hospitality. Congregations can easily fool themselves into believing that they are hospitable on Sunday mornings because their doors are open to all. That is a pretty passive message of hospitality![3] The other deception resides in congregational leaders assessing their members as "friendly" and, therefore, hospitable. However, what is experienced as "friendly" in a congregation often really means friendly to the friends and family who show up regularly, not friendly to those who occasionally or rarely appear at worship services.

Hospitality includes actively inviting as well as more passively welcoming. The invitational role suggests that all congregational leaders need to "hit the streets" to engage people with listening ears, audible voices, and a visible presence to develop relationships with others in the community. Inviting people into meaningful relationships is part of Christian hospitality and relational evangelism.

Once those relationships have blossomed into a meaningful partnership in ministry and people accept the invitation to join a worshiping and serving congregation, another dimension of genuine hospitality is to wonder how the congregation has now changed. New lives added to a faith community means new gifts present and available to shape the ministry and spirit of the congregation. Incorporating new people into a congregation is not a one-sided process of influencing the lives of new people without the larger community also being influenced. Learn about new people and who they are as individuals and households, their gifts, passions, values, faith, and more. Ask, "Who are we now that these new people have become part of our congregation? How are we now different as a congregation?"

 Who are we now that these new people have become part of our congregation?

Perhaps this is a reason some congregations avoid moving beyond their walls into the larger community. Some people don't want to be changed, don't want their patterns and comfort zones nudged. To be hospitable and truly "friendly," people need to invite as well as welcome, to be influenced and changed as well as to influence and change others through faith in Christ Jesus. In this sense, the evangelism of Christian hospitality requires the constant cycle of repentance and renewal, for the kingdom of God has drawn near through the welcoming of others in Christ.

Most congregations will describe themselves as a friendly congregation (I do recall one man who had the courage to say out loud, "No, we are not a friendly congregation."). On one specific occasion I challenged a congregational staff that had just described the congregation as friendly. I told them that a few years before I had preached in that same congregation. Between worship services I stood in the middle of a very large fellowship space with people all around the edges engaged in friendly conversation. I don't think there was anyone within ten feet of me. No one greeted me. No one pursued a conversation with me. No one. I was able to be extremely frank with the group because the senior pastor had already alerted me that there was an unrealistic self assessment by the congregation that it was "friendly," a view that the senior pastor did not agree with but, as the relatively new senior pastor, had difficulty challenging.

Biblical hospitality has a long and revered history. It generally involves food, sharing a meal together, and has even been known to include washing the feet of guests, the kinds of practices identified through the Four Keys. To eat together is a sign of covenant, of forming a relationship of commitment to one another. God joins Moses and the elders in a covenant meal in the form of "burnt offerings" (Exodus 24:3-11); the Gibeonites are spared their lives as they trick Joshua and the Israelites into having a common meal. Once these foreigners had become guests, the Israelites could no longer kill them as intended and instead had to establish a treaty with them (Joshua 9:1-27). The Wisdom of God treasures the lives of the simple by inviting them to a banquet

(Proverbs 9:1-6). The Bible concludes with the people of God awaiting the most hospitable invitation imaginable, to the marriage feast of the Lamb of God (Revelation 19:9). And to this very day people still commit themselves to one another as they break bread or tortilla or injera. During the Great Depression some opened their homes to offer food to those who had no roofs, no kitchens, no pantries. Impoverished Nicaraguan women did similar feats in the 1980s by rising before dawn to share their limited resources and prepare a simple meal over an open fire for foreigners promoting peace in the midst of the nation's civil war. Others have done similar deeds of service by offering food for the hungry and shelter for the homeless in any time and any place, a testament to the prophetic vision of Scriptures like Isaiah 58:7.

Congregational members can still do similar acts of hospitality by greeting visitors with a smile and handshake, directing them to an information booth, nursery, restrooms, and worship and fellowship space (such gestures and action steps are enormously important, for first impressions influence whether or not people return for another visit), sharing the peace of Christ with persons unknown, joining together at the Lord's table, then walking out together to become better acquainted, perhaps over a church supper or a meal in one's home. In fact, there are older adults in the church today who grew up assuming that all newcomers to a Sunday worship service ended up in congregational homes for a Sunday meal. Christian hospitality that opened one's home to another is the only life they knew (the kind described in the Acts of the Apostles). Some congregations are reigniting that spirit of hospitality today by providing regular or seasonal (i.e., Thanksgiving, Advent, Christmas, or Lent) meals that bring people of different generations together to enjoy a table grace over soup and sandwiches and caring conversations.

Immanuel Lutheran Church in Eden Prairie, Minnesota has sought to reignite Christian hospitality through an innovation that they call, "Invite a Friend to Church Sunday." Granted, "Invite a Friend to Church Sunday" hardly seems to be an innovation! In fact, when it is suggested to other congregations—even with great enthusiasm and delight at its novelty and punch—people laugh and roll their eyes in disbelief that this could be the ticket for innovative change in evangelism and faith formation. The general response of the impatient and disbelieving crowd: been there, done that.

However, underneath this well-worn evangelism tool may, in fact, be something quite novel, especially if "church" means not the Sunday morning worship experience but the more intimate setting of the church in the home. It's what Catholics have promoted quite clearly since Vatican II as the "domestic church," and what Protestants have described as the "first church" of an infant or child.

Once we substitute this new definition of church (the third of the Five Principles), a new horizon of meaning emerges. The goal is not to begin with a faith forming invitation to a congregation. The focal point is a more personal, non-threatening, and, for many, a more significant relationship. It centers on Christian hospitality, one of the ancient Christian practices, and one of the arts of the Christian faith that is worth renewed attention in the American Christian landscape.

Fortunately, people are once again lifting up the Christian practice of hospitality. Diana Butler Bass, one of the great researchers and authors on congregational renewal, does so in her book *Christianity for the Rest of Us*. There she references Henri Nouwen's words on hospitality in the book *Reaching Out*. However, when Bass writes about hospitality, she reflects nearly exclusively on the hospitality of a congregation. This is legitimate, but it is also limiting and definitely not the focus of Nouwen's work, nor is it the heart of biblical or historic Christianity's experience of hospitality. When the attention to the art of hospitality is on the congregation, its greater gift and practice have been minimized and reduced to an institutional category instead of the intimate, vulnerable, and grace-filled arena of the home. In fact, Nouwen's own biblical examples of hospitality are all domestic examples, from the hospitality of Abraham and Sarah with the three strangers, the widow of Zarephath with Elijah, and the two disciples on their way to their home in Emmaus with Jesus.[4] When Bass references a biblical example for a congregation's emphasis on hospitality, she uses Acts 2 without noting that it was a Christian practice of the home as well as the public temple (see Acts 2:46).[5]

For numerous reasons, the home in recent decades has been overlooked and devalued as a treasured expression of the church and a place for evangelism.[6] Because of the diminished role of the home and the inflated role of the congregation, it is quite understandable that when one hears, "invite a friend to church Sunday," one automatically thinks congregational instead of domestic church and congregational instead of domestic hospitality. Once that error has been corrected, another location for meaningful hospitality and evangelism can emerge.

Immanuel Lutheran Church made that correction and used the theme "invite a friend to church Sunday" for the Season of Epiphany to encourage the members and friends of the congregation to open their homes to others with Christian hospitality. Each Sunday the worship service and sermon focused on the Christian practice of home hospitality through one of the Four Keys: hospitality and caring conversations; hospitality and a devotional experience; hospitality as service to one's neighbor; and, hospitality that comes alive through gracious rituals and traditions like welcoming people in and lighting candles.

The Four Keys represent what might be called the embedded faith practices of the church, the essential and irreducible practices that are configured in numerous ways to establish the larger and historic practices of the church, practices like Christian hospitality. Pastors Paul Nelson and Susan Weaver helped the worshipping congregation imagine the kinds of caring conversations appropriate for a home meal with guests, recommending conversation starters, suggesting specific resources like FaithTalk® Cards,[7] and encouraging table graces as a devotional piece that would be appropriate for a meal hosted in a Christian home. Having people over for a meal and social exchange is itself a valuable form of service. Such practices recall rich and gracious rituals and traditions associated with inviting people into one's home in a culture that has become more sterile in its forms of home hospitality.

Following an explanation of the theme and how to fulfill the theme through the Four Keys, Nelson and Weaver gave the worshippers placemats printed with conversation starters and table graces. The congregation had even made hundreds of fortune cookies that contained more conversation starters as a way to keep the experience both playful and doable. The people were sent out with these resources and the weeks of preparation provided during worship services to join one another in each other's homes for a meal and Christian hospitality. The plan was to begin with invitations to each other's homes as a way to make the experience less threatening, on the assumption that most people in America are far removed from the tradition, practice, and comfort of this kind of home hospitality. The assignment to offer Christian hospitality in the home with one another had been communicated weeks before to prepare participants to schedule the Sunday meals. Before homes could be opened up to the larger community, organizers thought it would be wise for people to practice with each other the custom of Christian hospitality. They hoped that through such practicing, parishioners would become more comfortable inviting others into the church in their homes and offer meaningful, Christian evangelism in a world hungering for a place to belong, to feel safe, and to rest in God's love.

During the week that followed the assignment of practicing Christian hospitality in the home with one another, Pastors Nelson and Weaver contacted people from the congregation to learn how the experience had gone. What worked? What delightful experiences were there to record? What didn't go so well, and how could the congregation learn to do a better job of teaching Christian hospitality in the future?

They learned, to no surprise, that the practice of home hospitality was a challenge. Many had not participated. They learned that the experience was also a blessing to many others who did accept the opportunity. People observed that sitting around a table goes much further to connect people to one another than simply sitting in the same pew. There were accounts of shared laughter, stories, struggles, and support, the joy in just being together. Pastor Nelson observed, "This was also a profound growing experience for those who led prayers, devotions, and caring conversations in their homes." One person reported back, "Faith wasn't being done for me by the Pastor. I was doing it. I was leading; I was praying. I could do this." Pastor

Nelson's evaluation continued, "Perhaps the greatest lesson that came out of this was that it needs to be done again and again. This is not a novel, one-time seasonal event to fill the calendar. It is a vital practice in living out our faith, of helping people turn their homes into church, and stepping up as spiritual leaders."

 Sitting around a table goes much further to connect people to one another than simply sitting in the same pew.

Now that the congregation has committed to Christian hospitality in the home, Immanuel Lutheran has been able to enrich their Faith Group (small group) ministries. They have been able to help people see that they can lead prayers and devotions, begin a caring conversation, and connect their faith more and more to their daily lives in and through their homes. The congregation continues to develop materials that equip people to do the Four Keys in simple and practical ways, for example, by providing weekly handouts that promote the Four Keys for use during the following week. Staff, councils, and committees use these same recommendations as a way of expanding their use. The leadership has made it a priority to connect Sunday worship with daily discipleship, the kind that happens through Christian hospitality. This emphasis has touched lives. One mother who acknowledges that she is not a singer shared with the congregation her nighttime ritual with her children, which includes prayers, blessings, and the singing of a lullaby. She sang the lullaby to the congregation, and as off key as it was, it was perceived as beautiful because people could see how such a simple and personal gesture can make a big difference in a family's faith life.

With this focus on Christian hospitality in the home, Immanuel Lutheran as well as other congregations are rethinking how to do ministry with small groups, Bible studies, church committees, youth and family groups, and other ministries that can happen in intimate and faith forming settings of the home. For example, one way of incorporating new members into the life of the congregation may be to invite them to the homes of established members instead of putting them on a committee. Other congregations are conducting more congregational experiences like youth groups, Bible studies, and even council meetings in homes. People readily acknowledge that this change in setting also changes the ambiance and dynamics of the gathering. It personalizes, it deepens, even cherishes the Christian moment in ways not experienced otherwise. People recognize as significant the practice of being welcomed into someone's abode, especially when it includes sharing the gift of life through food together. It exudes a spirit of joy and humility, the kind that is kindled by the love of God in Christ who is ever present in those occasions to welcome, to reconcile, to renew, and to save lives.

The previous examples, nonetheless, still draw upon the magnetism of the congregational community. While such examples do represent the evangelism of the Christian faith, they do not in and of themselves reach out to those not yet drawn into congregational settings. However, it is a start, a modeling within the congregation to help members reach out beyond the congregational setting and be a strategic outpost for Christ's love in the larger communities around congregations and Christian homes.

The challenge for congregational leaders willing to address Christian hospitality in the home is significant, for all these practices are easier said than done. The whole idea of opening one's home to a larger audience besides close family and friends is a bit foreign to many—if not most—in our culture. The kind of evangelism that includes Christian hospitality in one's own home is countercultural. Many feel hard pressed to find the time and the energy to entertain family and friends with a meal in their home. Sometimes a coffee shop or a park can serve as an alternative "home" location, especially when meeting at a particular home is simply inconvenient. In whatever way the spirit of home hospitality is established, given the biblical warrant and the missional benefit of this Christian practice, it remains a focus on evangelism worth considering.

With increased practice and ease, Christians can be empowered and equipped to do hospitality evangelism beyond established congregational communities. They can invite children, grandchildren, friends, neighbors, colleagues, and others into the church in their homes to experience the care and presence of Christ through conversation, a table grace, the breaking of bread, and a hospitable spirit that reflects the words of Paul, "Welcome one another, therefore, just as Christ has welcomed you, for the glory of God." It is all part of the faith forming practice of Christian hospitality, like inviting a friend to church, the church in your home.

Milestones as Outreach

Another congregational ministry that is rich with possibilities for outreach into the community is Milestones Ministry (see pp 00-22 in "From Christian Education to Faith Formation" for details on Milestones Ministry). A milestone is a meaningful, memorable moment. Milestones Ministry embraces a meaningful, memorable moment as a moment to experience the presence and grace of God in Christ. Foundational to all Milestones Ministry is baptism or dedication, depending on one's faith tradition. This initial milestone symbolizes the lifetime of occasions to be reclaimed by and reclaim the saving work of Christ in one's life and for the world. Other milestones in a congregation can include beginning Sunday school, first communion, receiving a Bible, confirmation, weddings, and funerals. Milestones experienced in the church in the home include birth, getting a pet, moving to a new home and neighborhood, getting a new job, losing a job, marriage, and divorce. Not all milestones are happy moments; yet milestones framed in Christ reveal their deepest meanings and hopes.

A milestone is a meaningful, memorable moment.

Once a congregation understands that "the church is the church only when it exists for others," then they see their entire ministry including Milestones Ministry moments in the context of outreach. For example, parents and grandparents whose children are disconnected from a church experience like Sunday school at times feel the tug to do something spiritual for their kids. A congregation that continues to present itself as "their" congregation will discover numerous opportunities to connect with adults wanting something more for themselves, their friends, and their families.

The beginning of a new confirmation class can be an occasion for a family not involved in the life of the congregation to join a milestone event that focuses on "uniting teens and parents through the Christian faith" (creative descriptions beyond traditional labels like "confirmation class" can help people see possibilities not otherwise imagined). Congregations that have confirmation programs are often amazed at how many and which people show up for the new year of confirmation. Confirmation is a Christian tradition that still has influence in some families not otherwise very connected with the life of a congregation. The beginning of Sunday school, getting a Bible (including storybook Bibles for younger people), blessing school backpacks, beginning middle school, blessing a first driver's license, moving to a new home, first/next job, marriage, divorce, birth, adoption or guardianship of a child, unemployment, and retirement can all be promoted for the local community year after year. Invitations to such events can be posted on signs on the congregational property and become more personalized through the invitations of neighbors, friends, family, co-workers, and classmates.

Over time, people in the local community will begin to assume that that congregation down the street is their congregation. Peter Eckermann is a youth and family leader in Australia well versed in the Vibrant Faith Frame. He tells the story of being part of a new congregation, Mawson Lakes Community Church. For eight years the congregation had been intentional about connecting with people who may have no church background. At a recent Christmas service, Peter approached a man he had not seen there before and asked if he was a visitor. The man responded, "No, I'm not a visitor. This is my church. I come every Christmas." It is a simple and modest account, but one that indicates how people can begin to see a sense of connectedness, one that can grow over time through other milestone moments besides an annual Christmas service.

There are particular milestones that do draw the surrounding community to the local congregation, milestones such as Christmas and Easter services, weddings, funerals, and dedications or baptisms. It is worth the congregation's leadership being aware of serving numerous people who would not otherwise "darken the door" of a church building. Instead of guilting people for not showing up more (the Christmas and Easter crowd), leaders can take these opportunities to send people out of the worship experience with resources to continue to nurture the Christian faith in their daily lives. Send people out with caring conversations related to the particular milestone, devotional pieces that can continue to lift up a milestone as an ongoing faith formation experience, service ideas to revere life related to a milestone moment (including donations to use on behalf of others), and simple rituals and traditions that remind people of God's presence and love in their lives. All of this can be offered by a local congregation to nurture the faith life of people in the surrounding community, even—or especially—when the people are not in a church building.

There are also milestone moments that are perfect for the ministry of the church in the home. The announcement of a pregnancy, a new baby coming home from hospital, a person coming home from hospital to convalesce, a new neighbor next door or down the street: these are a few of the occasions that make it easy to connect with others in a time of need or celebration. Offering a meal along with a printed or handwritten table grace may be all that is needed to start a relationship of care and faith with another. Giving the gift of a Christian resource for new parents or a periodic visit to people convalescing at home are simple gestures of faith and good will that go a long way to communicate Christ's love in word and deed.

Congregations can easily provide resources to assist people in this valuable outreach. Worship books contain examples of prayers for a rich variety of human experiences. Many congregations offer training with concrete resources to help caregivers reach out to those in need. And of course neighbors, friends, family, and many others in addition to those making home visits on behalf of the congregation can use those resources. An example is *For Everything a Season: 75 Blessings for Daily Life*[8], a resource that gives conversation starters, Scriptures, prayers, and other ideas that assist small groups in caring for one another with the rich treasures of the Christian faith. Once milestones in daily life have been identified as moments ripe for creative and supportive ways of providing people with the care of the gospel, countless opportunities, ideas, and resources will emerge within the congregation to respond to this form of evangelical outreach.

What follows are some examples of how to promote Christian evangelism through the life of the local community, home hospitality, and Milestones Ministry. Of course, it requires discretion and sensitivity to address different people with the love of God in Christ.

Here are some of the hospitality practices that assume that Christian hospitality is not simply a way to reach out to the unchurched or once churched. Many of us long for times of deeper faith-filled conversations that shape our lives over time. That time may be a family dinner that brings out the never before heard story of a grandparent. It may be a social gathering in which a young person affirms her or his Christian faith. It may be any number of occasions in which people explore and wonder about the treasured meaning and deeper issues of life. These are moments not to overlook in the midst of hectic and anxious lives. Consider some of the following suggestions for your life and relationships.

When guests arrive in one's home or congregation

- Begin with the attitude of Romans 15:7: "Welcome one another, therefore, just as Christ has welcomed you, for the glory of God."
- Treat people like royalty, as if they are children of God (see 1 Peter 2:9-10).

- Turn off work conversations (whether church work or office work), cell phones, computers, and televisions.
- Greet the guest(s) with words like, "Welcome! Peace be with you" (see John 21).
- With words and gestures, invite them in (make it clear you are happy they have come).

When welcoming them into the home

- Remove the awkward beginning of what the guests are to do by greeting them with a smile and handshake, suggesting a place to sit, taking coats and hanging them up, pointing to restrooms, and other gestures that help people "feel at home."
- Make sure they are comfortable; perhaps offer them something to drink or eat as an appetizer.
- In addition to the small talk of weather, sports, and busy lives, include stories that reveal personal values, concerns, and faith.
- Sing Christian hymns or praise songs (simple selections are important here). This can work especially well when children are present or during holidays like Christmas and Easter.
- If children are present, consider using a storybook Bible and reading a story with and for the children. (Adults can benefit from this, too.)
- If the group is older youth and adults, consider reading a favorite and uplifting Bible text (e.g., Psalm 100 or Galatians 5:22-25). Consider reading a Scripture passage appropriate to the season of the church year, calendar year, or people's situation in life (*For Everything a Season* has examples of Bible passages for a number of occasions).
- When using a storybook Bible, Bible passage, or devotional book, include the whole group of guests by asking one or more of the following questions:
- What did you hear in this story/text?
- What got your attention in this story?

- What questions do you have about this story/text?
- What do you give thanks for in this story/text?
- What does this story/text make you want to do?
- What prayers do you want to offer as a response to the conversations around the reading of the Bible story/text?

At mealtimes

- Ahead of time, inquire about your guests' food allergies or lifestyle issues (e.g., being a vegetarian) and have alternative foods ready.
- Suggest where people might sit at the table.
- If it is evening, light candles and say: "Stay with us Lord, for it is evening" (see Luke 24:29). For other times of the day, say: "Jesus is the light of the world."
- Before a table grace is offered, ask if anyone has any prayer requests.
- Offer a table grace like: "Dear God, we thank you for this time to visit together and to receive this gift of food, signs of your continued love for us. In the name of Jesus Christ, Amen."
- During the meal, engage in caring conversations, being attentive to your guests, their life story and concerns. You may want to use FaithTalk® Cards or the FaithTalk® apps or some other resource that introduces conversations in an easy and non-threatening way.
- The close of mealtime is also a good time to read a storybook Bible or a passage from Scripture.

When guests leave

- Remember that the word "Good-bye" is a contraction of the Old English phrase, "God be with ye." Consider words of blessing like, "The Lord bless you and keep you" (Numbers 19:6).
- After your guests have left, keep their life interests and concerns in your thoughts and prayers.

Welcoming the local community to the congregation by

- Having signs outside the church building inviting people in, not just in general, but around specific milestone moments. Make these invitations ongoing, using different and specific moments like the blessing of pets, of a new school year, of a new driver's license, of retirement, and the honoring of special days like Memorial Day, Labor Day, and Halloween. Invite the community to these congregational moments with the spirit that it is also "their church."
- Training members how to welcome neighbors, friends, and family to milestones that will bless their lives (inviting into homes as well as into congregational settings)
- Doing faith-focused civic milestone events in parking lots and parks, public places accessible to all to celebrate Memorial Day, Fourth of July, Labor Day, and Halloween
- Interviewing civic leaders to learn of the issues and needs of a community (remember, spirituality is a basic human need)
- Offering worship services that celebrate the gift of community and the blessing to serve the local community with God's love in Christ
- Being present at community events like parades and festivals
- Committing the congregation's efforts to serve the surrounding community and not just the members
- Encouraging congregational leaders to interview people in the community, especially the "invisible people" who are often overlooked.

2

From Christian Education to Christian Faith Formation

A congregational leader in children's ministry from North Carolina wrote the following story to me in an email:

> It was a surprise to me when one of the first grade Sunday school girls said to a boy in the class, "You don't come to Sunday school very often." The boy replied, "Well, my mom is sick a lot on Sunday mornings. She tells us to watch church on TV."
>
> The girl looked up from her coloring to make eye contact with the boy and said, "I'm sorry. You don't get to come and hear the children's sermon, pass the peace, sing, or go up for communion. One time my brother was sick. We had to stay home from church and Sunday school. My mom came right into my bedroom, and we had a Sunday school lesson right there. It was the best lesson ever! Maybe your mom could do that for you sometime."

From Christian Information to Christian Faith Formation

Over the years Christian education leadership in congregations has faithfully provided opportunities to learn God's story and the foundations of the Christian faith at different ages and through different programs like Sunday school, Vacation Bible School, innumerable Bible study courses, and new member classes. The goal has been to provide high quality events that draw people in and nurture their Christian faith. Leaders have typically assessed those educational events through attendance taking and sometimes through evaluation forms.

Yet the fundamental goal surely is not improved attendance or information dissemination in a classroom but lifelong faith formation of Authentic, Available, and Affirming—AAA—Christians who receive God's story of grace and live into that story day in and day out. That goal is realized as people are equipped and supported to bring the Christian faith into individuals' and communities' daily lives and larger world experiences. It represents the kind of active discipleship program that Jesus had for the disciples, an action-reflection model of training believers for the work of sharing the good news in word and deed. Once people move from receiving Christian education opportunities to promoting the larger work of lifelong faith formation and Christian discipleship, the focus shifts from a class to a community that practices its faith in a rich variety of settings.

Our little girl in the opening story gets it. It is hard to beat the impact of a faith-forming environment in the home. It can be experienced as "the best lesson ever." Faith enrichment moments include the generations together communicating and experiencing God's love in worship, in song, in a Sunday school class, in the home, and elsewhere. When the faith formation environment expands beyond classrooms and curriculum, both classrooms and curriculum benefits and a whole new horizon for Christian education opens up, one that includes cross+generational events, worship, family faith formation training, mission trips and a variety of other Christian faith practices. More traditional educational opportunities like Sunday school, confirmation classes, and vacation Bible school begin to involve parents and other mentors, the kinds of opportunities recent research and congregational testimonies show reach the desired outcome of trusting, knowing, and living the Christian faith for a lifetime.

Moving beyond the Heyday of Sunday School

Christian education flourished in the twentieth century, especially in the 1950s and '60s. It was modeled after the public school classroom and had well-prepared adult teachers, chairs neatly organized in circles or rows, and a formal curriculum developed with clear scope and sequence and provided by a trusted publishing source, often a denomination's own publisher. Sunday school teachers were nearly a profession unto themselves, some serving for decades at a time. Children and youth were sent to these classrooms on Sunday mornings to get education in Christianity, that is, to learn the stories of the Bible, and, at some level, to learn the piety and theology of the local congregation's denominational heritage. Children maintained friendship ties in Sunday school through high school. Since attendance was not mandatory, perfect attendance pins were celebrated, and proper religious socialization reinforced that good Christian families came to worship together regularly (meaning weekly) and the children attended Sunday school.

But that is no longer working, and perhaps it never did, at least as an isolated Christian education program. In fact, Sunday school originally was not designed for the churched home but for orphans and other children who had lost touch with an adult faith forming community. It was a children's evangelism tool. Perhaps Sunday school worked in the past because it was part of a larger faith eco-system that kept families, neighbors, and communities more closely tied to a Christian ethos where more citizens knew the faith traditions, understood and used the language of the faith, supported weekly "church nights," and otherwise promoted a culture in which Sunday school was one piece of a larger faith formation puzzle. Sunday school teachers and other Christian education leaders did a wonderful and faithful job over the generations, but their work was not accomplished apart from a larger community of faith.

The spiritual landscape of church and society looks very different today. It is not reasonable to assume that what worked a half a century ago will work the same way today. The very denominational structures that supported Sunday school have been in decline. The two hundredth anniversary of Sunday school took place in the 1980s without fanfare. By the end of the century, the average self-identified Christian could not name three of the Ten Commandments and did not know who gave the Sermon on the Mount. Regular worship attendance now generally means once or twice a month, and perfect attendance pins are a thing of the past. Worship attendance (let alone adult Sunday school or weekday Bible study) has become optional for dads, if they are in the family and faith picture at all. The Sunday school year has shrunk from twelve months to nine, and getting children to Sunday school through grade six seems a reasonable accomplishment. In some settings Sunday school has been restructured so that teachers divide up the assignments with many other teachers. That way they only teach a small portion of the Sunday school curriculum and have less contact with the students. Some congregations and larger judicatories pay only lip service to the whole Sunday school enterprise. Such different results are not due to poor teaching or poor curriculum. They are due to placing all our faith formation eggs in the Sunday school basket, rather than understanding it as having a supportive role to faith formation in the home.

The delightful and precocious first grader described above is an anomaly. The little boy and his mother are not. That the little girl could articulate the piety and practice of her congregation so well should not be surprising. She had experienced the home as a key component to receiving and learning the Christian faith. Her mom could teach the faith at home in a way that made it "the best lesson ever!" Her mom is equally an anomaly in today's church life in which parents rarely feel equipped or empowered to teach the faith in their own homes. Like the little boy's mom, most parents long ago became distanced from the Christian formation of their own children. Some would say that parents have walked away from their responsibilities. It may be more accurate to suggest that a philosophy of church life has undermined this faith formation role of parents by saying, "Bring your kids to us. We have the experts, the institutionally trained, informed, and inspired educators. You who are parents don't know enough."[1] That creed itself has become a self-fulfilling prophecy.

The Vibrant Faith Frame as a Twenty-First-Century Guide to Christian Faith Formation

Three decades of research on what truly influences faith formation,[2] along with the Vibrant Faith Frame, promote an alternative model of Christian education, one that gives more attention to the desired outcome of a living faith than to institutional numbers and attendance pins. Review the Five Principles through the lens of faith formation (the desired outcome of Christian education) and it reads like this:

- Faith is formed by the power of the Holy Spirit in relationships rather than by paper curriculum. (We are the curriculum!)
- Effective faith formation ministry partners home and congregation as a vital team instead of employing a hierarchical model that places parents and other caring adults in a subservient role.
- Home life makes an incredible difference in a child's ability to be inspired by the faith (and as an adult this child then inspires the next generation).
- A child (or adult) catches the values and faith of those around them by word and deed, not simply by lesson plans and data dispensed.
- To ignite and motivate the young with the Christian faith, surround the young with adults who live that faith and wake up hungering for it.

To put it simply, what we call the role of cross+generational faith formation, or different generations interacting as a community of faith, is a foundational contribution of the Vibrant Faith Frame. That is quite different from placing one or two adults in front of a group of young people for an hour to give a 25-minute Sunday school lesson (the average length of instruction during an hour of Sunday school). This does not mean that everything a congregation does needs to bring the generations together, but it does mean that cross+generational contact (meaning multiple generations interacting with each other as a community of faith) has much more to offer Christian faith formation than most of us in the church understand today. Nor does it mean congregations should discard Christian education opportunities in favor of parents teaching the faith at home. Rather, it means that the faith lessons need to be brought "home" and be discussed, lived, and practiced through the formative guidance of the Four Keys.

Surrounding young people with AAA Christians who are real (authentic), not sleeping on the job (available), and blessing the lives of children and youth in Christ (affirming), is essential for a viable approach to Christian education in a congregation. Nothing less will do. Nothing less will work. And children and youth actually desire it. Whether it is a father encouraging the faith life of his children in the home or a cross+generational Sunday school hour, the sharing of lives, questions, values, interests, and stories between the generations creates a stimulating environment to grow in the grace of God in Christ.

As a result of exposure to the Vibrant Faith Frame, two yoked congregations decided to change their Sunday school curriculum for the fall. The Four Keys they easily incorporated into the new curriculum, and the students came together for the Bible lessons as cross+generational "family groups" (beginning with fourth graders and including people in their 80s) every other Sunday. The study used groups gathered by ages on the alternate Sundays. Several weeks after the fall program had begun, the pastor polled the youth and asked if they would say that the new format is "better than before," "worse than before," or "about the same." None of the youth answered "worse than before." The pastor writes, "By about 2 to 1 (about 10 polled), they have responded "better" than before, and a couple of even said, "WAY better," citing how much they appreciate being with the older people of the congregation. This pastor also observed that many adults, especially older adults, expressed their appreciation for the opportunity to be in contact with children and youth. The pastor was wise enough to share this informal poll and its positive response with the congregation. Many of the adults were pleasantly surprised by the comments of the youth.

Another congregation struggled with the complaints by the youth that they were not supported by the older members of the congregation. The pastor asked for a clarification of this complaint, pointing out that many of the youth's activities were actively supported by and funded by these very adults. The youth responded that that was not their point; they wanted face-to-face conversations and other interaction with the older adults. (There is clearly biblical warrant for this. See 1 Thessalonians 3:10; 2 John 12; 3 John 14).

The youth proposed a cross+generational Sunday school hour. Unfortunately, the experience disappointed some of the older people. The logistics did not work out very well, for many adults ended up not having any children or youth in their groups. They expressed their deep reservations about trying that idea again. However, the youth came back with their own suggestion of having occasional cross+generational Sunday school hours between the middle school youth and an adult Bible study group and between the high school youth and another adult Bible study group. Their recommended formula results in six Sunday school sessions between youth and adults during the year. According to the pastor, that arrangement has been well received both by the youth and the adults. One of the joys of this alternate plan is that the youth wanted it and designed it. Once again, the adults were surprised by the youth's desire for meaningful contact with them.

A youth and family director wrote the following story that describes what happens when cross+generational faith formation in the home becomes a primary focus for a congregation's Christian education. This is a story of a confirmation parent who "gets it."

Jim attended the confirmation parent meeting at the end of August. He sat and heard about the confirmation program and all of the ways we encourage the students and their families to live a vibrant faith during the confirmation process.

I have observed Jim on more than one occasion in the sanctuary with his oldest son a half hour before worship began. So when

Jim stopped by my office recently I asked him about this practice. He reported that at the confirmation meeting he saw the sermon notes part of the program as an opportunity to spend time with his son. Their practice is to arrive a half hour early to observe and discuss the things they see in the sanctuary, and to read through the readings for that Sunday. They continue to discuss what is happening in worship throughout the worship service. I have sat behind them and can say that I have witnessed this quiet but important conversation happening between them during worship.

To hear Jim describe their meaningful ritual and tradition is life-giving for me. This particular practice happens in the church building, but I can imagine all the other times and places this father and son are able to discuss their faith outside the church building because of the experience they have inside the church building. Hearing Jim's story has helped me as a church staff member to realize how greatly a family's life can be affected when even one parent "gets it."

This faith formation experience bridges a traditional Milestones educational experience (confirmation) with worship and parent-child conversations. Together, these practices provide a rich experience in faith formation for multiple generations.

A Fresh Look at the Teaching of the Church

The Book of Acts perceives preaching and teaching as a seamless whole. While the church remained in Jerusalem "every day in the temple and at home [the apostles] did not cease to teach and proclaim Jesus as the Messiah" (5:42). Later, when the church was reaching out to the Gentiles, Paul says about his own ministry, "I did not shrink from doing anything helpful, proclaiming the message to you and teaching you publicly and from house to house" (20:20). At the end of Acts, Paul is under house arrest in Rome "welcoming all who came to him, proclaiming the kingdom of God and teaching about the Lord Jesus Christ with all boldness and without hindrance" (28:30b-31).

Preaching and teaching is what the early evangelists and missionaries did, but the categorical distinctions between preaching and teaching remained obscure. What was not obscure was the result of their efforts. "They devoted themselves to the apostles' teaching and fellowship, to the breaking of bread and the prayers" (Acts 2:42). It did not take long for an identifiable Christian tradition and subculture to emerge. Their sense of community and commitment was evident in that "they would sell their possessions and goods and distribute the proceeds to all, as any had need" (2:45). They gathered publicly and in homes. They preached, they taught, they prayed, they broke bread together, they served the needs of others, and the result was that "the Lord added to their number those who were being saved" (2:47b). Preaching and teaching both focus on learning the faith, living the faith, and the outreach of the church into the larger world. The New Testament church described in Acts and elsewhere had a particular way of life together that incorporated preaching and teaching, passion (Acts 4:31), commitment to one another, suffering with joy (5:41), and the growth of the church.

In the twentieth century, as the church became more institutional, programmatic, and expert-driven, it became easy to isolate Christian education from the larger way of life and outreach of the church. Christian educators using professional curriculum in congregational classrooms taught Christianity, thereby restricting the transmission of a tradition and subculture to a classroom. However, some in the church are repenting of reducing teaching to ideas rather than an informed way of living the Christian life. As one pastor describes her work in adult learning, "Part of what adult formation is focusing so heavily on now is getting away from the educational model and into the lived faith model and how we help people live out their faith. It is the whole discipleship piece."[3] That particular pastor is not against education. She is a former public school teacher. She just knows that presenting data in a classroom is not enough.

That distinction between Christian formation and Christian education affects children as well as adults. People like John Westerhoff and Robert Wuthnow recognize that the old school-instructional model is not the best way for the Christian faith to be passed along to others.

One study of adults and their religious learning observed that few of them remembered being especially curious about metaphysical questions as children and few of them recalled significant teachings that provided answers to these questions. They assimilated religion more by osmosis than by instruction. The act of praying was more important than the content of their petitions. Being in Sunday school was more memorable than anything they may have been taught. . . . the parents, teachers, and clergy who understood this best were the ones who created an environment in which spirituality was fully and deeply embedded.[4]

The Vibrant Faith Frame represents an understanding of passing on the Christian faith between the generations that is "fully and deeply embedded" in the whole life experience of people in both public and more personal settings. It encourages a faith formation environment that celebrates God's story of the universe that shapes the lives of individuals, households, congregations, communities, and larger world.

Milestones Ministry: The Entry to Adult Faith Formation

The Milestones Ministry from Vibrant Faith Ministries offers a gentle, non-threatening way to nurture lives of all ages in the Christian faith and serves as a template for other faith formation possibilities. It promotes faith formation consistent with the Vibrant Faith Frame and provides methods and resources for effective faith formation in and through the congregation.

A milestone is a meaningful, memorable moment in a person's or community's life. It can be anything from a birthday to a graduation, wedding, first job, retirement, being a grandparent, or moving into a new home. Milestones can be joyous events like the birth of a child. They can also be sad events like the death of a loved one, a divorce, or the loss of a job. Whatever the moment, what makes it a ministry event is connecting it to the love of God in Christ, that is, to mark the moment with the cross of Christ.

Milestones Ministry is a way to remember and live one's baptism, to connect with the faith journey immersed in baptismal promises and recalled in a lifetime of occasions to connect faith and daily life. The Vibrant Faith Frame is a way of being, perceiving, and doing life in Christ. Milestones Ministry in a congregation is a programmatic way for people to participate in the vision laid out by the Vibrant Faith Frame and to do Christian education with a focus on faith formation for all ages.

A fully developed Milestones Ministry event in the congregation includes four elements. The event: names it (the particular milestone moment), equips it (by providing Four Key practices to experience this moment as a faith milestone), blesses it (through blessings and other prayers particular to that moment), and gifts it (by giving a tangible item that helps recipients recall the milestone in their lives as a valuable and formative moment in the journey of faith). Congregational Milestones Ministry generally includes a cross+generational training for recipients, family, friends, and mentors followed by the celebration of the milestone in worship, and follow-up events to further nurture the Christian faith and learn how the Milestones Ministry event continues to affect their faith lives.

A primary goal of Milestones Ministry is to provide faith-nurturing events that become incorporated into people's daily lives in homes and communities through the Four Keys. One father shares a story that lifts this up in a very concrete way. Through his congregation's Milestones Ministry program, his family has begun to bless one another in the home. He writes:

> *For the last two years my wife and I have blessed our children before school and/or bedtime. We often use the words, "May the word of Christ dwell in you richly and keep you safe." We mark a cross on their forehead as we bless them. Infrequently, but sometimes, Rachel, age ten, and Robert, age seven, bless us back.*
>
> *On Friday after Thanksgiving we arrived at our home after an overnight away with family. We were rushing to get Rachel*

unpacked and then repacked for a Girl Scout lock-in event. We were running a few minutes late and I was rushing to get Rachel out the door and into the car. Robert, in my opinion, was slowing us down with, "Wait, Rachel, wait! I want to tell you something." As I waited at the door, Robert caught up with his big sister, reached up his arm, put his forefinger on her forehead, and as he traced the cross, said, "May the word of Christ dwell in you richly and keep you safe."

Wow. I thought about it later and determined that it wasn't just a blessing. Rachel and Robert had shared a bedroom for the last two weeks while some construction work was being done in Rachel's room. They had enjoyed the shared nighttime space. Rachel was planning on moving back into her room on Saturday. Thus, that Friday night marked the end of that two-week, sister-brother bonding experience. The blessing that Robert gave his sister before she went out the door was also a way of telling her that he was going to miss her. Is there a better way to show or tell someone you are going to miss them?

The milestones here could be variously understood. Rachel was going to a lock-in milestone. Robert and Rachel were moving back into their separate bedroom spaces. Robert was going to miss his sister, and Dad had a meaningful, memorable moment that he may never forget. What held it all together as a Milestones Ministry event is that, literally, the cross of Christ and the word of Christ were placed into the middle of the occasion. Robert's family had become fluent with blessings at bedtime and good-bye times. A family ritual had become so ingrained in the home that a seven-year old could serve as family priest at a tender yet hectic moment in the family's life. It is often through Milestones Ministry that the Four Keys become a family habit that blesses and nurtures the home and those who come in contact with the household members.

The experience that Dad witnessed, Robert initiated, and Rachel received probably would not have happened had their congregation not been trained in the Vibrant Faith Frame. The same is true for the congregation of Mike and his family (described below). Both congregations had participated in a Vibrant Faith conference and experienced the Vibrant Faith Congregational Training. The congregations have learned about and do a variety of Milestones Ministry events like baptism, beginning Sunday school, first communion, getting a Bible in third grade, confirmation, and graduation from high school. Some of those events and practices the congregations have done for generations. Others are being added as the congregations become immersed in the Vibrant Faith Frame, events like beginning middle school, blessing a new driver's license, or entering into retirement.

Milestones Ministry in a congregation concretely teaches people like Robert and his family how to live the Christian faith, and how to live the story of God's creating, redeeming, and sustaining work. All elements of the Vibrant Faith Frame are present in this approach to faith formation. The Six Locations of Ministry have an important role in Milestones Ministry because they not only serve the faith nurturing environment of home and congregation for people of all ages, they direct the church in the home and congregation into community, culture, and all of creation. A blessing of a young person's first car keys links faith in the home with responsible driving in communities and teaches values not always endorsed by the broader culture. The Milestones Ministry event of preparing for and blessing a mission trip connects the love of God at home to the ends of the earth, and to the care of the earth itself. Milestones Ministry lives out the Five Principles by explicitly connecting the church in the congregation with the church in the home. You see this in people who have become more comfortable with conversations about God, with Bible reading and prayer in the home, with serving others in the neighborhood and world, with supporting the Christian tradition of mealtime prayers, saying "good-bye" with a Christian blessing, or practicing various Christian holiday traditions in the home during Advent, Christmas, and Easter. This relational, person-to-person focus of the Five Principles creates a training ground to reach out to others beyond the congregation. The Four Keys structure those faith practices in age-specific ways and at different stages of life. The desired outcome for this ministry is once again AAA disciples, people like Robert, his sister, and his dad who are growing in grace to be authentic, available, and affirming.

One adult interviewed in a focus group about the impact of Milestones Ministry in his congregation said, "I think these kids talk about Jesus and the church and what they learned at church, at school with other kids. You can't even imagine where that might go."[5] That observation led a dad to talk about his daughter's congregational Milestones Ministry experience of entering middle school and recalling that she is a child of God. Each student was given a mirror to put in his or her school locker. The mirror had on it the words *imago dei*, meaning the image of God, to remind the students that they are created in the image of God. The dad said of his daughter, "She was able to tell her friends about what those words meant. Some of them thought it was cool and some of them wondered about it, too. She as a sixth grader had some foundation and was able to share her faith."[6]

Milestones as Evangelical Outreach

Milestones open up conversations that can lead to evangelism in a public school hallway and in our own homes. Once the congregation understands its ministry being to serve the surrounding community then everything it does is also for the community and not just for members. The milestone of beginning another school year can be a Milestones Ministry event for the whole community. One church I know is across the street from a middle school. The congregation made a ten-foot banner inviting all the students across the street to a blessing of the backpacks, along with family, friends, and neighbors.

Whether it is for a blessing of the animals or to mark the beginning of a year of Sunday school, congregations can find creative ways of inviting the entire community, not just the kids who have been going to Sunday school in the past. The same is true for most any other Milestones Ministry event: invite everyone. Those who accept the invitation and come experience the love of God through that milestone moment. Another step is to invite other area congregations to join such community efforts. It helps alleviate fears of competition and presents an important sense of Christian unity in the community.

One campus ministry uses Milestones Ministry to identify twenty-five different occasions in the life of college students. Each occasion is represented with a Milestones Blessing Stone, a small piece of clay with an image on it symbolizing a different milestone. Sermons and prayers include these milestone moments. Students come in during the week to get a stone that connects with what they are going through at the time, and are also given a bowl in which to place the stones. The campus minister has noted the great success of this ministry, both in terms of connecting with students and the depth of that connection. One student was the victim of violence and describes her experience with the campus ministry's Milestones Ministry in the following way:

> *The Milestones Ministry is teaching me many positive things about how my life as a college student relates to my faith. Recognizing the various milestones that I am going through is allowing me to celebrate the highs and lows in my life. An important thing that I have learned from Milestones Ministry is that the low points in life need as much recognition as the high points because our struggles allow us to gain strength and wisdom. Sharing my milestones with others has given me support and encouragement. It has also given me the opportunity to support and encourage others during the milestones of their lives. Each milestone in our lives, good and bad, is a blessing from God.*

Whether it occurs in the neighborhood or on a college campus, Milestones Ministry reaches out to people needing God's story to be part of their story, their identity, and their way of life.

Follow-Up Work Makes Milestones Ministry Effective Faith Formation

After congregational members and community residents attend a Milestone Ministry event like giving Bibles to third graders, the next step in outreach is checking in with the participants. For example, a month after the Bibles have been introduced, after the cross+generational group has learned how to use the Bibles, and after the Bibles have been given in worship, get together the third graders, their families, and other people who participated in the Milestones Ministry event to see how those Bibles are being used as a faith nurturing resource in the home. Substantive faith formation checks in with people and helps leaders to understand what is needed next. What's working? What's not? What questions have arisen? Where are the success stories to tell that can encourage others? Responses to such questions deepen the impact of Milestones Ministry as well as doing effective faith nurture and outreach into the local community.

Do Less, but Do it More Thoroughly

One of the great gifts of the Vibrant Faith Frame is helping congregations focus on what makes a difference for lifelong faith formation and outreach versus what feels like an obligation to offer year after year. Once the faith formation leadership has shifted from a focus on classroom attendance and programs to lifelong faith formation that emphasizes cross+generational contact, the home, and faith practices as ways of living into God's story of creation, redemption, and sustaining, one of the results is to desist from offering ministry that is "a mile wide and an inch deep." Most congregational leaders know this tendency and feel burdened by it. Congregations try to do a bit of everything to reach the masses, but then don't go deep (for example by failing to check in with people and to offer continued care). Lifelong faith formation instead encourages congregations to do less. Whatever is done, follow up contact is critical so that what is taught actually sticks with people and their faith practices. It is more important to go deep into people's faith formation journeys than it is to offer lots of educational appetizers that do not transform lives over time.

Milestones Are Not Just for Kids

The beauty of Milestones Ministry is that it presents a clear structure and endless possibilities for bringing faith into the home and into daily life. One congregation created "Celebrating Our Elders: A Milestone Celebration of Lives of Faith." It honored those members in the congregation who were ninety years old and older. Three of them were interviewed as part of the sermon, including a father interviewed by his son, the president of the congregation. Moving stories and examples of faith were given by those interviewed. For the children's message in the worship service, the children delivered special cards to the elders present at the service. The cards had been prepared the week before at a cross+generational service event.

At the Celebrating Our Elders event, a milestone occasion was *named*, the community was *equipped* with stories of faith to build up the body of Christ and practice the Four Keys, the elders were *blessed* during the worship service, and they were *given a gift* to recall the moment. That particular milestone emphasized the importance and wisdom of the oldest adults. That can happen by them being the ones honored at the milestone moment, but it also needs to happen through them participating in others' milestone events, for example when children receive a Bible, enter Sunday school, or go to school for the first time.

After taking a workshop on ministry to married couples during a VFM summer workshop, one congregation decided to begin a new tradition. Each Valentine's Day, the congregation now holds a dinner for all the married couples in the congregation. The Parish Hall is beautifully decorated, and teenagers of the congregation help serve. On the table are cards with two conversation starters: "Share the story of your wedding day," and "What has been most important in making your marriage work?" After the dinner, everyone goes into the sanctuary of the church and each couple comes to the altar in turn and renews their wedding vows. It is powerful to have a couple that has been married for a year or two renew their vows and then watch as a couple that has been married sixty-five renew their vows as well. This new tradition moves younger and older adults alike.

The "little secret" of Milestones Ministry is that even when it is a child's milestone, the focus is truly more on the adults in the lives of those children. It is the adults in the children's lives—and not a short-term educational event in the congregation—that have the long-term impact on children's faith formation. In a story told in more detail below, it seems likely that neither Mike's wife nor the congregation would ever have gotten Mike to an adult Christian education class, but he did come to several. They were just called Milestones Ministry classes and the focus was not on Mike (a relief for him, to be sure). Mike came because he loved his children and wanted to support what was good for them, even "a little religion" and moral training (a typical motivation for not-so-churched parents to come to something that equips the Christian faith). Milestones Ministry is one of the most successful adult Christian education opportunities happening in the church today, even when—or especially when—it is a child's milestone that is being recognized. Granted, it is not a very challenging biblical curriculum, but the vast majority of adults in America are not ready for that anyway. Let them get their feet wet with children's storybook Bibles and then see where they can go.

At the heart of Milestones Ministry are the Four Keys of engaging in caring conversations, devotions, service, and rituals and traditions that bless people's lives with the Christian faith and bless the lives of those around them as well. More than one dad or mom has commented, "I can't believe how much those Four Keys have changed my family's life." When people see the Christian faith affecting and changing lives, there is a new way to evaluate or think of Christian education and faith formation: how it is making a difference in people's lives.

Congregational Faith Formation that Changes the Life of the Home

Part of Vibrant Faith Ministry's coaching of congregational staff includes an on-site visit with members of the congregation to discover directly from them how the Vibrant Faith Frame is or is not working in their lives. On one occasion, a woman emailed her thoughts to her pastor because she could not be at one of those evening gatherings with the VFM coach and congregation. She wrote:

> *I wish I could be there . . . I'd love to talk with him [the VFM coach], but I'll be teaching my cake decorating class. Would you pass this along?*
>
> *One thing that I have found amazing about this Milestones Ministry has been the unexpected impact on Mike. As a "fallen Catholic," he's always been "iffy" about church, faith and God. He's even ventured to say that he doesn't believe in God (only to me . . . not the kids, thank goodness). With the tentative steps I have taken with the Milestones Ministry, I've seen a change in Mike. He's not swinging a cross around and smacking people with a Bible, but I see a very subtle change.*
>
> *One night at dinner while using the Faith Talk Cards, Mike actually said, "So Max, what do you think Jesus would want you to do about that?" I about dropped my fork!!!*
>
> *When something happens that he knows I've been praying about, he'll say, "Have you been praying??"*
>
> *Mike's more open and supportive of our activities at church, even when we have over-extended ourselves. He's willing to bring Max to Children's Choir practice even when I can't. It's a very subtle change, but it is a very obvious one that I've been praying for and seeking for over 14 years.*
>
> *As a congregation, we are focusing so much on our children right now, but I didn't even realize that the changes I was making in our home were affecting the one person I pray daily for God's presence to stir in his heart! Please thank [VFM trainer] and share our story. I know I'm not the only family like this . . . and it's so encouraging to see progress. I have regular conversations with God about "his time" and "my time" with respect to Mike's spirituality, and it likely will never be exactly what I expect . . .*

but I see God's influence and presence more and more in Mike's actions. I don't know if I'll ever see him in a regular church service, and I'll eventually come to peace with that. Seeing the snippets of God's presence in him is more than enough for me.

Thank you.

Yes, like this wife and mother, many others would love to see someone regularly be a part of Sunday worship. With Mike, that appears to be unlikely for now. However, Mike's wife now sees the kingdom of God at work in her life and her home in ways she had not before, and she is delighted. What has changed is that instead of berating Mike to make him show up at God's house (a pattern that his wife confessed to in another email), God has been making Mike's digs a pretty comfortable home. The wife attributes it to Milestones Ministry's model of nurturing faith in the home.

FaithChests®

Making FaithChests® is a concrete way to emphasize Milestones Ministry as an important part of a congregation's life. FaithChests® are those very tangible boxes, sometimes beautifully made as a piece of wooden furniture, that become a visible reminder of the home as a place to nurture the Christian faith among friends and family. Often made by woodworkers in the congregation, these home altars and chests keep within them the faith memorabilia and resources to talk about faith and life at home.

FaithChests® not only equip homes with resources and a visual reminder of the holy ground of the home, their construction in the congregation provides opportunities for cross+generational service together. One congregation paired boys with men to construct such chests. Side by side the men and boys worked, laughed, discussed personal and global issues, and prayed for those who will receive the chests. Months and years later those events are recalled with statements like, "Remember the time we made those FaithChests® together and the stories we told about faith in the home?" It just doesn't get any better than that.[7]

Milestones Ministry as a Template

Clearly, there are other forms of congregational faith formation besides Milestones Ministry. More important than the specific endorsement of Milestones Ministry are its implications for effective congregational faith formation: it provides outreach into the community; it recognizes the critical step of follow-up by checking in to learn how the event affected people's lives; it helps congregations focus on the essentials and let go of the rest; faith formation involves all generations and at its core gets into the hearts and minds of adults who then, through their relationships, modeling, and teaching, also get into the hearts and minds of children and youth; it needs to affect not only individuals but households, the church in the home that is the outposts ministry for the work of the congregation; and, finally, visual reminders of the Christian faith in the home like FaithChests®, crosses, Christian art, and other artifacts of God's word for people's lives (see Deuteronomy 6:6-9) are all part of providing helpful Christian faith formation in the congregation.

Other Forms of Christian Faith Formation
A Midweek Family Program

Congregations have developed a rich variety of means to help people grow in their Christian life and faith understandings. One congregation has developed a weekly program called "Building Bridges" that equips parents with experiences and resources to comfortably and meaningfully pass on the Christian faith to their children—and vice versa. A basic tool of the Building Bridges program is the Faith Box, a simpler form of a FaithChests® that is made out of a cardboard box. Its presence in the home and the faith resources it contains, like a storybook Bible, helps put Christ and the Christian faith in the center of the family's life. Building Bridges assumes that if you want people to do something regarding their faith life in the home, then you need to practice it with them in the congregation.

Andrea Fieldhouse, the developer of Building Bridges, writes:

> *Parents are champing at the bit for more knowledge about God and ways to have and raise faithful children. We make them promise lots of important things at baptism and then we don't help them do it! They just simply don't know how, and certainly don't feel safe. Our job is to model, encourage, equip, hold their hand, affirm and help them practice faith!!! BUT, the programmatic part is delightfully easy – it's God's story and our story and prayer and music and play, what could be more easy!*

As with every other aspect of the Vibrant Faith Frame, Building Bridges is not rocket science. Once congregations honor the role of the home in faith formation, it is simple to create settings and experiences through stories, prayer, music, and play that allow families to be families of faith.

One parent describes Building Bridges in the following manner:

> *I sometimes struggle with coming up with creative ways to talk about God with the kids, and Building Bridges really helps with that. For instance, I learned that a fun activity was to read a story from our children's Bible, and then have the kids draw a picture of the story. Anna loves art and has had a fun time with this – and whether she realizes it or not, she is learning about God at the same time.*

Building Bridges is also a way for us to do a faith-oriented activity as a family. In today's hectic world, it is all too easy for families to forget to talk about God and their faith on Monday through Saturday, so it helps us to keep it a priority in our lives.

One mother writes:

> *For me, the strength of Building Bridges is that it brings families together to learn how to talk about faith in an easy and fun way. I also think that for young children especially, using the same language over and over to reinforce learning is so*

important. By learning about God and Jesus' love together we can reinforce the learning at home by telling the stories using the same words, recalling the hands-on activities, and remembering our experiences at Building Bridges. There is so much benefit to the way the stories are presented. By allowing our children to touch, act out, and truly experience the stories, they make a better connection to them.

These are real families with the typical challenge of time. That same mother goes on to state:

As a family, we are very busy. It is easy to go through each day without taking the time to focus on our ultimate parenting goal of raising loving, faithful children who love and know God and strive to follow the example that Jesus' life gives us. By making a family commitment to participate in Building Bridges, we are showing our children that our faith is very important to us and to our family. We are also guaranteeing that as a family we will set aside two to three hours a month (program plus at-home activities) to focus on developing our faith. In addition to the time spent on Building Bridges, there are natural conversations that arise related to a story that we talked about or through daily experiences.

She also gives a good example of a strength of this kind of cross+generational faith formation, one that challenges the more recent pattern of child-centered Sunday school. It is the kind of observation made by other parents in the Building Bridges program:

It might just be my 5 year-old son, but after Sunday school, I take the sheet that they send home and [by asking him questions] I try to understand what he learned at Sunday school. It is like pulling teeth and I never get very far. This isn't to say that the program isn't great, but it is hard for us to find things to talk about. I ask questions like "So, you learned about David and Goliath today, huh?" However, after Building Bridges, I know everything that he learned and how he learned it, so our conversations can go more like this, "You did a wonderful job thinking of things that God uses angels to tell us. What was your favorite part about Building Bridges tonight? You liked painting the angel's wings? Well, I really liked when you said that God wants us to remember not to give in to temptation. Where did you learn about temptation? Oh, you remember it from the Lord's Prayer. Let's say it together."

A Host of Unique Ideas Coming Out of Congregations

Once congregations see that the desired outcome of Christian education opportunities is not attendance at a class but a life worth living in Christ, then the faith formation possibilities are endless. Instead of just talking about the faith, people can live out the faith with and for one another.

One confirmation class in Raleigh, North Carolina ends each class session with a blessing. The adults bless the youth and the youth bless the adults. Another congregation gives the newly confirmed youth each a scrapbook that contains notes from family and friends filled with words of encouragement, faith, and wisdom.

Congregations are exploring other ways to lift up the importance of AAA Christians in the faith formation of the larger faith community. Similar to the Milestone Ministry event Celebrating Our Elders, one congregation periodically honors a AAA adult during worship services by bringing him or her to the front of the worship space and recognizing and praying for that person, and giving a gift to memorialize the moment.

Small group ministries have emerged as part of many congregations' faith formation work over recent decades. Whether they are Bible study groups or fellowship groups, those groups can be grounded in full-blown faith formation practices of the Four Keys. They can see their purpose as larger than supporting each other but branching out as AAA adults to the needs of children and youth and the cares of community, culture, and creation. Everything can become faith formation material for small group ministries.

Mission Trips and Other Servant Events

Mission trips can change people's lives, but recent research has seriously questioned their long-term impact on participants.[8] True, they can reinforce the same old patterns, such as realizations that, "Thank God I don't live here." But even then, at least these trips give us pause to ask: What really matters? What does grace and mercy and faith look like for others? What does it feel like to do something for others? What does a sense of accomplishment and new skills tell us about what we can do in the future? How do others experience God? Mission trips raise a number of good issues, questions, reflections, memories, and one hopes more than a few faith-forming experiences.

For Pastor Russ Sorensen, his latest mission trip was different than the eight he had been on before. The difference was not the location in Mexico or the task of building a Habitat home. The difference was the intentionality of the trip to be reflective and faith forming as well as exhausting and exhilarating. The difference was the decision to "Four Key" the trip with the centerpiece being a devotional every evening, one that encouraged reflection and caring conversations about faith and service and the needs of the world. It was a way to grasp the whole experience, and not just to admire the good deed one was doing.

Pastor Sorensen's group was composed of thirteen high school students and four adults. The evening time allowed the participants to have candid conversation about how the experience affected them. For Pastor Sorensen, the result was unlike any other mission trip. The Sunday morning testimonials when the group returned home were profound and eloquent. One youth said, "I usually complain about a lot of stuff, things that are not convenient or whatever, but I did not complain about one thing that week." There was an attitude of gratitude that deepened the experience. They talked about the dedication service for the house that was built. The father who had helped with the construction and was part of the family receiving the home knelt down on his knees on the cement floor and rededicated his life to Christ in front of the team who had helped build the house. The youth had never seen anything like that before, and Pastor Sorensen vowed never again to do a mission trip without the Four Keys to guide the experiences in such a way that the presence and word of God would be central to all that happened.

Mission trips can be very positive experiences. With cross+ generational storytelling, worship, service, and a communal tradition of the Four Keys, there seems to be a greater chance that what happened on the trip will not stay on the trip but return to shape the participants' lives for years to come.

When asked to address the faith component of the Habitat for Humanity experience, a youth and family director reflected:

> *I never knew why my mission trips were so much more successful than my youth and family ministry throughout the regular calendar year. Ah ha . . . it is because my mission trips follow the Four Keys to a "t" . . . before I knew what the Four Keys were. Often I have youth come back from college to talk to the congregation and the one thing that they mention is . . . 'remember that mission trip? Yep . . . it is and was a life changing experience. I will never forget it!'"*

The Four Keys simply name the faith formation that the church has already been doing so well over time.

A Tip for the Faith Formation Journey: Bring a Prayer and Action Partner Along

The goal of Christian education is not banking isolated information, but forming faith. One way of applying this principle is to use prayer and action partners. At the end of an event, have people identify what it is they want to explore in their life of faith (generally an example of one or more of the Four Keys) and commit to it with a prayer and action partner.

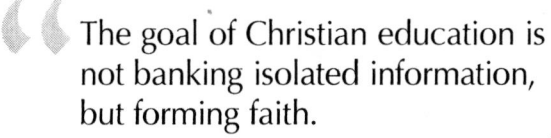

> The goal of Christian education is
> not banking isolated information,
> but forming faith.

That partner hears and supports the planned activity. That person may also challenge whether the activity is realistic. To commit to a new pattern of hour-long devotions each night before bedtime may be more of a statement of enthusiasm than reality. A partner can also: pray for the person and the desired faith practice; check in periodically to see how the journey is going; and can ask what adjustments need to be made. In this way, a class or event never quite ends with the final session or hour. It continues to shape a person's faith journey as people apply the learning to their lives.

A Final Word

The move from Christian education as a school-instructional program to Christian faith formation reflects a focus on discipleship, following the way of Jesus into the world. Since the time of Jesus and the New Testament church, this happens as people receive the gospel message of God's creative and redeeming work of God in Christ. Lifelong faith formation is foundationally built upon the work of the Holy Spirit to make that divine work a reality in people's lives today. That reality includes living the faith, what historically has been referred to as "yielding to" or being "obedient to" God's word. The Christian faith formation introduced in this chapter builds on the biblical and historic study and the practice of following Christ into God's world to serve, heal, reconcile, and save.

3

WORSHIP AND PREACHING

This chapter is not written to reinvent worship or promote one approach over another. It offers a slice of the worship and preaching pie that can be savored by Christians of many diverse tastes. Regardless of worship traditions, musical preferences, or theological orientations, the Vibrant Faith Frame can help us focus on specific, meaningful, and worshipful possibilities. The Vibrant Faith Frame intends to equip Christian disciples for their daily encounters in the larger mission field. Worship and preaching likewise have this intention, at least in part. Therefore, while this chapter will not define appropriate or best practices in music, worship styles or liturgies, or preaching used in worship, it will approach worship and preaching with an eye on the cross of Christ, with a spirituality aware of God's presence in the world, and with attention to Christian hospitality.

The Vibrant Faith Frame and the Worship Life of God's People

However worship is conducted in a local congregation the Vibrant Faith Frame has a contribution to make. Reflecting on the Vibrant Faith Frame for the ministry of the congregation, one pastor commented on "how deeply this pervades all of what we do and so it is in the back of my mind while I'm writing sermons."[1]

In other words, the Frame orients one's thinking while imagining and planning congregational life, including worship and preaching. Worship, however and whenever it happens, addresses a context for ministry that takes one beyond the confines of a congregation (the Six Locations of Ministry). Christian worship envisions the life and outreach of the church as a cross+generational community that does more than bring people together in a sanctuary on occasion (the Five Principles). The spirituality or "training in righteousness" (2 Timothy 3:16) involves foundational faith practices. Notice how the Four Keys are implied in the charge given by Paul to Timothy in 1 Timothy 4:11-15.[2] The 1 Timothy 4 passage conveys a training in righteousness through "speech and conduct, in love, in faith, in purity" (verse 12). The outcome of congregational ministry is first and foremost Christian discipleship (forming AAA Christians) and not simply congregational membership. As the pastor stated, this "pervades all that we do." The Christian faith intends to be a gift for the whole of the Christian life and for all that God has created. The Vibrant Faith Frame assists congregational leaders in keeping that greater goal in mind.

The Four Keys as the Centerpiece

Worship and preaching shape and direct daily life through a worldview in which the grace, mercy, and peace of God in Christ, and not death, sin, and judgment, have the last word.

The Four Keys place God's living word into our daily activities as we receive God's grace and guidance for life as well as when we extend God's grace and guidance to others. That reality, what Jesus called the kingdom of God, comes to us through the kinds of conversations in which we participate, the devotions of our lives (including public worship on a Sunday morning), who and what we serve, and the rituals and traditions that go beyond words to convey meaning and hope in our lives.

We see this worshipful interaction of the Four Keys present throughout Scripture. I mentioned 1 Timothy 4:11-15 earlier. Another example of the ubiquity of the Four Keys is in the temptation story in Matthew 4:1-11. The devil wants Jesus to worship him, but Jesus will have no part in that. He engages in a direct conversation with the devil. It may seem odd to consider it caring conversation (both caring and careful toward the kingdom of God), but Jesus' rebuke of the devil is just that. It reflects the perspective of Colossians 3:17 that speaks of teaching and admonishing each other, and that, too, conveys conversation filled with care for people's lives. Caring conversation is honest, true to the Christian faith, and intended to edify the church and all people. Jesus uses his words to such an end. Jesus' conversation is devoted to the word of God present in Scripture. Interestingly, even the devil knows Scripture. What is missing is the heart and soul of the Scriptures directed to serving and praising God, not any other power or glory (including our own). Jesus confirms the second Key, a devotional life, by noting that we live "by every word that comes from the mouth of God" (verse 4b). Our lives are to be devoted to God. Instead of serving the devil and all that stands apart from the kingdom of God, we serve God, which identifies the third Key. Such service of God includes serving all that God creates and loves, for "those who love God must love their brothers and sisters also" (1 John 4:21b). It is also evident in the Son of Man who comes identifying the sheep on the basis of their service to others, through which they serve the Son of Man (Matthew 25:31-46). And, finally, the temptation story has the fourth Key of rituals and traditions woven into it throughout. It begins with Jesus fasting, a Jewish and Christian tradition. He enters the wilderness, symbolizing the location of renewal and identity formation. He ends up on a holy mountain, reminiscent of Moses and his encounter with God. The foundational practices of the Christian faith serve as a means both to receive the story of the gospel as well as to guide the life of the gospel community.

In one particular congregation that went through the Vibrant Faith Congregational Training, when the pastors were asked to identify the Four Keys and reference them in subsequent sermons, the senior pastor had some misgivings about this. It was not the way he had been trained. As a result, the trainer invited him to call him for help in exploring the Scriptures during future sermon preparations. However, the pastor never called. After some weeks, the trainer contacted the pastor and asked why he had not called for the promised help. The pastor responded that it was not so difficult after all. He routinely found the Four Keys in the Bible now and was confident he could help worshipers do the same thing in their own lives.

Just as the Four Keys are present in the life of the Bible, they are present in the life of Christian worship. The responses between worship leaders and the worshiping congregation offer a sample script for faithful and caring conversations. To say, "Praise the Lord," or "peace be with you," is language appropriate not only for the worship life of the Christians but also for the daily life of the faithful.[3] The public worship service includes the Scriptures and prayers that serve as resources for the devotional life of the home. The Christian practice of service is everywhere in and around public worship. As people walk into the gathering place they often see posters or tables or booths promoting one form of service or another. The needs of people's lives are listed in bulletins, included in prayers, and presented in sermons. Worship is also filled with rituals and traditions, liturgies of word and gesture, such as hands folded, hands outstretched, or hands raised. As one Baptist pastor said, "Don't be fooled, we all have our liturgies that shape Sunday worship. It may not be written, but it is expected. Worshippers have an idea of what is coming next in the service with or without a written liturgy." How we greet, when and how we read Scripture, the use of music are all forms of Christian rituals and traditions variously practiced by different denominations, including the nondenominational congregations. All of that is to be brought out of the public worship space and planted in the spaces of our daily lives.

Naming, claiming, and valuing the Four Keys in worship helps people reinforce and reproduce these faith practices in their daily lives and therefore equips people for their ministries in the larger mission field as AAA Christians. For example, my colleague and friend Paul Hill has recently become a grandfather. He has come up with a "liturgy" for greeting his new grandson. When he first sees his grandson, he says, "Hello James Malcolm Hill, child of God, I am so grateful to see you!" What beautiful liturgy and Christian affirmation from grandfather to grandson. A young adult leaves a worship service and practices his own faith-filled tradition of turning off the radio when he gets back into his truck. He does so because he wants to focus on what he has just heard and experienced in the worship service and to give attention to one thing he can apply to his life. One time after worship he simply reflected on what a gift it was to serve others. Recently, he had helped an older woman whose car had a flat tire on the highway. In that moment of turning off his truck radio after worship, reflecting on the word of God in worship and preaching, and recalling with joy a recent opportunity to serve another, he had just concretely identified all of the Four Keys: caring conversation with a person in need, devotional material from the worship service, service to the person with a flat tire, and rituals and traditions of turning off his truck radio after a worship service.

The very practice of reflecting on worship after the service is a valuable Christian tradition. It is a practice that links the worship service to the larger life of a Christian. Such a practice says, "Worship is not a time out from life. It shapes life." For a child the tradition might be discussing the children's sermon message with family on the way home. A woman practices this tradition when she leaves worship by reflecting on a Bible passage that was the focus of the sermon. She wonders to herself how that text might guide her as she has a performance appraisal meeting with an employee at work that next week.

It is good to keep the Vibrant Faith Frame in the back of one's mind as that quoted pastor does. It directs our imagination of what is and what can be. It focuses our attention on the eternal in life, not simply that which is passing away. It affects how one prepares for and leads worship.

Five Contributions of the Vibrant Faith Frame to Worship and Preaching

The Vibrant Faith Frame contributes to worship and preaching through the following five elements:

1. Worship and Preaching are a Way of Life
2. Worship and Preaching are Missional
3. Worship and Preaching Involve Dialog
4. Worship and Preaching are Cross+generational
4. Worship and Preaching are not Just Public Events: They Occur in the Home, Too

Worship and Preaching are a Way of Life

The second of the Five Principles states, "The church is a living partnership of the ministry of the congregation with the ministry of the home." That principle promotes an integration of public life with personal, everyday experiences that take place in a more personal setting, described as the ministry in and through the home. (The concept of "home" here means much more than where a person lives. It stands for all those intimate relationships and settings that are life-shaping and give a sense of stability to one's life.) The public and the personal together give us a larger sense of who we are as individuals, households, and larger communities. Christian worship affects the whole of one's existence.

The Apostle Paul exhorts the church in Rome "to present your bodies as a living sacrifice, holy and acceptable to God, which is your spiritual worship" (Romans 12:1b).

Public worship is not only something that we hear, see, and voice in a particular religious gathering, but an experience that sends people out with lives nourished by God's word.

The worship in the congregation should be reflected in the worship of our lives as "living sacrifices." Public worship exists, in part, to shape people's daily lives—their conversations, behavior, thoughts, and pursuits—expressed through the foundational faith practices of caring conversations, devotions, service, and the rituals and traditions of individuals, households, and larger communities.

The "spiritual worship" identified in Romans 12 takes place in many ways, including during a Sunday service. It was the last Sunday before Christmas (the Fourth Sunday in Advent for some), and two worship events took place in the space of a few minutes. The first was in the middle of the worshipping congregation. A somewhat anxious yet beaming couple and their four-week-old daughter sat down next to Elaine, an older woman sitting alone. During the worship service Elaine leaned over and said, "That's a good baby. She must not be too old." The young mother showed the infant to Elaine and noted the baby's age. The second happened moments later when a two-year old in the same row waved to her older sister in the choir up front. Elaine then invited the two-year old onto her lap to look more closely at the baby. Before that service, Elaine had not known either the young family sitting to her left or the two-year old to her right. But there they all were, in the middle of a children's Christmas pageant, three generations of love, life, and Christmas joy blending together.

It was clear to the young mother that Elaine had interest in her baby, and so the mother asked if Elaine wanted to hold the baby. Elaine responded eagerly. Elaine took the baby in her arms, looked longingly into the young face, and proceeded to tell her own family story. Elaine had been married 62 years but was alone now. Her husband had died three years ago. Elaine observed how she loved babies. She had had her own and now had eleven grandchildren and four great-grandchildren; all lived far away. The young mother listened intently and was glad that she had shared with Elaine the bundle of love of her life. In a few moments another pageant of love and life and faith unfolded: the good news was read, sung, and acted out in the front of a community of worshippers, and in the middle of the congregation the message of a baby who came into the world was experienced on a whole other level.

In this situation, worship as a way of life and for the whole of life was presented in the front of the worship space as well as in the middle of it. Both realities are worthy of the attention of worship leaders. In this story, three generations were present with their bodies as living sacrifices prior to, during, and even after the worship service. Public worship can help people connect the dots between their conversations and care for each other with the awareness of living in the presence of God and for the glory of God. Who knows how those generations may have deepened their relationships to each other after the worship service. A widow and grandmother far from her own children could certainly use the contact of "family" closer to her home. A young parent could certainly benefit from the wisdom and loving attentiveness of a grandmotherly person. A two-year-old could always feel welcomed by greetings at worship in subsequent weeks to feel her own sense of belonging. All of these possibilities reflect the impact of worship for all of life.

Later in that same worship service yet another message was introduced to the worshippers. On special occasions, the congregation has what it calls "Hand in Hand Moments," times for people in the congregation to tell their faith stories as a part of public worship. Such story telling brings the Christian faith lived daily alongside the faith lived in and through the congregation. For this congregation, the two arenas of living the Christian faith in home and congregation are to go "hand in hand." On this occasion, a three-generation family stood to tell their story about a family Christmas tradition reinstated the year before. The youth and family director prefaced their account by noting how these "Hand in Hand" stories are part of the life of the homes of the congregation, narratives that give examples of Christian faith practices like faith conversations, devotions, service on behalf of others, and Christian rituals and traditions.

The mother introduced their story by acknowledging that Christmas is a special time for many reasons, some joyous some sad. Christmas family traditions help people celebrate the joys of faith and life but also the sad times of loss, whether it is recalling the death of a loved one in the past year or after many years. She went on to say that Christmas traditions help people deal with things like divorce, something that she had experienced over a year ago. That recent history of deep pain and loss led the family to create a new Christmas tradition. A particularly helpful new tradition came from the Spirit of the Lord through Grandma the year before.

Grandma reignited the value of family Christmas traditions by developing a new family event that, she hoped, would help get the generations through the season following her daughter's divorce. She had her ten grandchildren plan a family Christmas pageant to perform for the larger family. All the grandchildren got a part to play, even the four-year old who preferred to play the part of a clown instead of an angel. After the family performed the pageant among themselves on Christmas Eve, they also did so at a local nursing home to a captive audience of about fifty residents. On that occasion a grandson who was just learning to play the trumpet led the family in a Christmas hymn, starting and continuing by playing off key. It all worked, anyway, with great joy and merriment.

Grandmother also spoke at the Hand in Hand moment during worship. She talked about the value of family traditions at Christmas and went on to acknowledge that this year, while the full pageant did not happen, the family did gather to sing hymns together to make the season complete. Grandma concluded by saying that this was a way to bring the family together in a new way and to bring Christ back into their Christmas celebration. Three generations of family were present and visible at the Hand in Hand Moment to offer in public worship a humble retelling about how a family Christmas tradition provided a precious moment in the midst of a sometimes painful season. Mother's and Grandmother's words translated the love, life, and message of Christmas from a family context to the larger arena of worship, worship celebrating the baby Jesus and the joy, meaning, and peace he brought on earth.

Another example of "spiritual worship" was woven into the same morning's worship.

This family story shared during a worship service occurred in a congregation that regularly taught the importance and implementation of basic faith practices. Part of that instruction comes through a worship resource called *Taking Faith Home*.[4] This resource weaves biblical texts into each of the Four Keys: a daily Bible reading, a memory verse for the week, a blessing to share, and a table grace for the week.

Using the *Taking Faith Home* worship resource is one concrete way of how to bring the worship life of the congregation into the daily worship life of individuals and larger households.

Congregations who use *Taking Faith Home* often introduce it through sermons or children's messages. Someone introduces the various possibilities presented in the piece, encourages people to use them in their daily lives, and then sometimes pastors and other congregational leaders follow up on another occasion by contacting worshippers to find out how Taking Faith Home affected their Christian faith in daily life. Researching the effect is an important element of spiritual care, for giving examples of how Taking Faith Home has made a difference in people's lives can enrich public worship. Providing Taking Faith Home inserts in worship bulletins and teaching the importance of their use is a way to emphasize and experience that worship is a way of life.[5]

The benefit of Taking Faith Home extends not only to those gathered for public worship, but to those offering and receiving pastoral care during the week. One pastor wrote that the Taking Faith Home led to one of the best homebound member visits he had ever had. When it came time in the visit to have Holy Communion he asked the woman he was visiting if there were any particular Scripture readings that she had been thinking about. She took out the Taking Faith Home resource that she had received earlier along with the Sunday bulletin and CD of the worship service, and said that one of the daily Scripture readings led her to struggle with her feelings that had been hurt by a friend. She told how she worked through forgiving her and renewing the friendship. This conversation also led to another about her son who had died when he was a young man. She was able to talk about her grief. The Taking Faith Home resource offered the kinds of options for reflection and, in this case, the time to prepare for those conversations, that made it a helpful tool for this pastor's devotions and conversation with a shut in. It connected the worshiping community on Sunday with a smaller community of worshipers on a Thursday afternoon.

Worship and Preaching are Missional

Some congregations have a sign at the back of their sanctuaries to be read as people leave worship. It states, "You are now entering your mission field." Other congregations place in their worship bulletins a message that identifies the ministers of the congregation as "all the members of (name of congregation)." Both of these messages communicate that Sunday worship time is part of a larger whole of living the Christian faith in God's larger world.

The church does not exist for itself. It exists for the world that God loves. That is the theological foundation for the Six Places of Ministry (from individuals and homes to culture and all of creation). That is also part of the message in the rear of the sanctuary, "You are now entering your mission field." Christian worship and preaching are not just for the committed follower of Jesus, but for those who are opposed to Christianity, for those who are indifferent to it, for those inquisitive about Christianity, as well as for those who almost accidentally become exposed to Christian worship because of a family or friend's milestone in life (milestones like baptisms, dedications, weddings, or funerals that often bring in people who would not otherwise participate in public worship). Through such occasions, worship becomes a form of evangelical outreach to the community.

The challenge for a missional church is to address everything from atheism to the false gods that tempt everyone. When a pastor hears, "Oh, that was such a nice service," that worship leader can legitimately wonder if the comment really meant, "Oh, pastor, worship today made me happy; it inspired me to feel good about myself; it didn't upset me, it didn't challenge me, and the message reinforced all my cultural biases." In a culture of individuals accustomed to comforts and "having it their way," a legitimate question for any Christian worship leader to ask is, "When does Jesus ever say to his followers, 'Pick up the cross and have a nice day?'" Isn't the message rather, "Those who want to save their live with lose it, and those who lose their life for my sake, and for the sake of the gospel, will save it" (Mark 8:35)? Jesus goes on to say, "Those who are ashamed of me and of my words in this adulterous and sinful generation, of them the Son of Man will also be ashamed when he comes in the glory of his Father with the holy angels" (verse 38).

In our likewise "adulterous and sinful" generation, there are a number of challenges for the church to be present for others. Current cultural religion (understood by many in America as Christian) says that religion should be kept private. But biblical Christianity knows otherwise. The Lord's Prayer does not include the words "me" or "I," only "our" and "us." The New Testament church preaches and teaches publicly and from house to house (see Acts 20:20). Cultural religion wants to make life into a "success story" filled with the honor and prestige of financial success. But biblical Christianity understands honor and success quite differently. The apostles left a council that had just tortured them and "rejoiced that they were considered worthy to suffer dishonor for the sake of the name" (Acts 5:41). Here the successful ministry of the apostles led to torture and suffering, not huge bonuses. Cultural religion wants people to "get ahead." Biblical Christianity wants people to follow. Cultural religion says that the church shouldn't talk about money. Biblical Christianity knows that Jesus talked more about money than prayer for he knew that "where your treasure is, there your heart will be also" (Matthew 6:21). Cultural Christianity teaches people to pray for their friends and family. Biblical Christianity says, "Love your enemies and pray for those who persecute you" (Matthew 5:44). Cultural religion says, "God helps those who help themselves" (actually from Benjamin Franklin's *Poor Richard's Almanac*). Biblical Christianity suggests a much different attitude: " 'Blessed are you who are poor, for yours is the kingdom of God'" (Luke 6:20). Cultural religion says we should fear the stranger, those who are different from us. Biblical Christianity knows that it is from strangers that Sarah and Abraham are promised a child in their old age (Genesis 18); and it is a stranger who enters into a home, breaks bread with disciples, and opens their eyes to the Resurrected Lord (Luke 24).

The list of contrasts between cultural religion and biblical Christianity can go on. As it does, one major theme recurs: cultural religion is not interested in living and dying for the world God loves. Biblical Christianity hears the call to do just that. Biblical Christianity is missional, always reaching out to those not yet living in and through the gospel of Christ Jesus. Cultural religion does not experience this joy of God-inspired sacrificial love. As a congregational worship leader prepares for worship services, it is good to ask oneself whether the message in word and action reflects the outward and reconciling move of the gospel or the more closed and inward move of self-preservation promoted by cultural religion.

The worship life of the church gets the word of God to journey with worshipers as they enter their mission fields. It is not enough to inspire a worshipping community without the intent of bringing the passion of God back out into the larger world of people's lives and God's care. One of the simplest ways of doing this is to provide recommended faith practices for worshippers to take with them into their daily lives so that they can continue to worship God through prayers and Scripture reading, faithful conversation, loving acts of service, and the traditions of the faith that remind them who and whose they are, people created to love God and love neighbor.

One congregation that has been trained in the Vibrant Faith Frame has taken its weekly bulletin and structured the weekly announcements through the language of the Four Key faith practices. Topics for caring conversation include information about the worship practices of the congregation, upcoming events, and information about the Christian life. The bulletin contains a variety of information in this section, material that is suitable for after-worship conversations. The section of the bulletin listed under devotions identifies a wide variety of concerns in the congregation that can be lifted up for prayer, including the list of hospitalized and shut-in members, and local and global issues. The list of Scriptures used in worship also provides meaningful devotional material for the week. Service includes a description of a number of ways the congregation is currently or could be engaged in serving the community and world. The financial stewardship of the congregation is lifted up in this section as well. Rituals and traditions incorporate the celebrations and remembrances in the life of the congregation and in the home lives of the congregation.

This congregation has effectively created a consciousness for worshipers that helps them see their lives, their values, and their activities within basic faith practices. That consciousness also structures the bulletin in such a way that it just might get read more. The announcements in the bulletin give people something to pray and discuss. Now they can pray the bulletin and make some of the information contained in the bulletin the stuff of daily conversations. Congregational leaders fear that people consider the information in bulletins, newsletters, websites, and other media outlets to be irrelevant to them. Now it is relevant in a new way. It encourages people to exercise their priestly calling and pray for new members, for the next mission trip, for the youth event, for the need for Sunday school teachers in the fall, for the community fundraising dinner for a family that experienced a tragedy, and for the next staff and board meetings. Through this strategy, this congregation highlights and exercises its missional work outside of the weekly worship service.

Another congregation did a sermon series on the Four Keys and ended by giving each home a "faith tool bag" that included conversation starters, ten ways to pray with two dice to help choose which prayer to use, a Four Key explanation sheet, and a Five Principles bookmark. Not only did people report on the positive impact of these practices on their home life, some individuals even picked up extra faith tool bags to give to neighbors, friends, and family. This offers a perfect case of how the home and congregation can partner in ministry through worship and preaching to do the outreach of the church.

Yet another congregation emphasized the Four Key practice of service alongside of public worship during the Lenten Season. Each week the worshippers did a different activity: they wrote Valentine cards and sent them to shut-ins, created cards for the sick and hospitalized, made a welcome book to new members with personalized notes from current members, sent letters to college and graduate students, and made Easter cards for students and staff in the after school program.

Other service activities included bringing food and cleaning supplies for distribution as part of the offering. Again, the feedback was positive, with thank you cards coming from the recipients of the congregation's thoughtful care.

Still another congregation used a worship series to focus on honoring the service of people in the community: medical workers, school teachers, police and fire department employees, and others. Each week the congregation identified one particular service group, recognized and prayed for them in worship, and gave them thank-you cards from the congregation for their service. With the theme of "God's work, our hands," cross+generational groups of worshippers went out into work places in the community—places that had agreed to receive this ministry—and blessed people's hands for their service to others.

Another way to see worship services as outreach is through those milestone moments like weddings, funerals, and dedications or baptisms that bring in family and friends to worship. Some of those folk have not been in worship since attending the last milestone for a family member or friend. Instead of waiting until the next milestone gets them through the congregational church doors, recognize that the home is church, too, and invite them over. Send the worshippers out of the wedding or funeral service with the word of God in the Four Keys. Create a Taking Faith Home piece appropriate to the moment. Let people experience God's presence after the worship service is over; see the Appendix for examples of handouts at weddings, funerals, dedications, and baptisms.

After funerals and memorial services one congregation distributes a handout that begins with an explanation of the Four Keys. The introduction states, "[W]e seek to send these key faith practices home, so that the presence of God is known not just here . . . but also in our daily lives of being the church sent back out into the world." It is clear to the pastors of this congregation that grief and the need for a living faith does not end with the conclusion of a funeral service. They see the funeral service not as a conclusion but as part of a person's faith journey through grief.

At a funeral service for a man named Warren, the pastor added a Four Key sheet to the bulletin. One of the caring conversation starters read, "One aspect of Warren's love for the church and of his faith that I never want to forget is . . ." People left the worship service with at least some sense of Warren's faith story. Now that understanding can serve friends and family as they go deeper into some of Warren's story after the funeral is over. Scripture and prayer were also part of this Four Key sheet. A reflection time about serving the world around us, just as Warren had, incorporated memorial requests. This funeral service provided a ministry tool to reach out to people whether or not they would be worshipping with the congregation the next Sunday. The word of God was brought "home" to people, giving them other opportunities to be blessed by the living word of God and to have a reason to return to this or another congregation for more. Who knows how these invitations to reflect upon faith at the time of someone's death can affect other people's faith life.

Weddings are another opportunity to reach people of all ages, especially those young adults who less frequently connect with Christian faith communities. A pastor did a wedding service for his niece and her fiancé. As part of the sermon, he gave them a Four Key resource in the form of a letter to use on their honeymoon, a honeymoon devotional written just for them. The Four Key honeymoon letter began:

> *Dear Jarrod and Lydia,*
>
> *Gloria and I are delighted by your love for each other and also your love for our Savior and Lord Jesus Christ. We pray you have a relaxing and memorable honeymoon. Don't bother to think about us, just know we will all be thinking about you two with big smiles on our faces.*
>
> *Love, Uncle George and Aunt Gloria*

The letter went on to give them conversation prompts related to their wedding day and marriage, Scripture, prayer, and service ideas for their honeymoon week, and it helped them establish new family traditions based on the Christian faith practiced in the home. The uncle then made the same Four Key piece available to anyone who wanted to use it as a way to join the couple on their "spiritual honeymoon." There was definitely some humor and play with this as the uncle made it clear he wanted to help the couple have great honeymoon experiences. At the same time, people left knowing that they could continue to experience a worshipful connection to the couple in the days ahead, a connection that gave everyone God's word for their daily lives, whether or not they returned to the next Sunday services. The Vibrant Faith Frame assumes that congregations can no longer simply wait and hope that people will reenter their doors for public worship. Especially today, it is important to bring the word of God to people. Pastors and other congregational leaders can then prayerfully hope and anticipate that lives will be blessed by such outreach and that people will eventually return for more.

Worship and Preaching Involve Dialog

Since "faith is formed by the power of the Holy Spirit through personal, trusted relationships" (the first of the Five Principles), Christian worship necessarily reflects a spirit of dialog. Whether it is formal liturgy, call and response in worship, a congregational "amen," or a spontaneous "alleluia," there is a give and take in relationships and in worship. The dialog takes place not only in the execution of worship but also in the preparation. Therefore, worship preparation that connects with the worshippers by listening to and asking good questions about people's experiences, ideas, and questions (a form of doing congregational and community research!) is valuable. The dialog can continue when people return to worship the following week to talk about the experiences they have had during the previous week.

Some clergy meet periodically with the youth of the congregation or with an adult Bible study group to get their "read" on the upcoming Sunday texts. What questions do they have about the Bible passages? What issues do they want explored in the sermon? What experiences in their lives connect with the texts in a way that they want bridged?

One pastor has begun using an email list of a men's Bible study group and one of college students and gets feedback from each of these groups to inform sermon preparation. On another congregational staff the children's and youth ministry directors help the senior pastor to use the congregation's Facebook page and to blog to get feedback from various generations, especially the young, to help in sermon preparations. The use of Facebook, blogs, and tweets may be a strategic way to get the generations to interface over texts. Numerous pastors have bemoaned the difficulty of getting senior high youth and adults of various ages together at the same time to reflect on Scripture passages and themes for worship and preaching. A challenge now could be to find ways to get the generations together by using social media to create the desired cross+generational conversations.

Such worship as dialog starts long before the worship service begins. Knowing the importance of Christian adults in the lives of children and youth, one pastor is committed to speaking with at least six children a day. He listens, asks questions, and learns from them. On numerous occasions what he learns finds its way into his preaching and prayers in worship. His commitment to being a cross+generational leader includes the voices of children and youth in worship. Their voices are heard in song, in Scripture reading, in other forms of worship leadership, and in being quoted in a sermon.

Not only children and youth need to be heard and responded to, so do the elders. Arnie is an octogenarian who routinely has caring and deeply religious conversations with a local pastor during their workouts at the gym. Arnie heard a radio evangelist talk about judgment and the next day asked the pastor about it. Arnie wanted to know what would happen if church simply erased any distinction between right and wrong. Then he wanted to know how the pastor understood the law of God. Arnie likes to get into the deeper questions about what is most important in life. He wants to know and often asks, "What's the purpose of life?" Sometimes Arnie's own answer to his question is "love," but the pastor challenged that to be more than an occasional emotion and become a commitment to serve one's neighbor. On other occasions Arnie would answer his own question by saying, "We are here to learn." But then the pastor said, "But Arnie, learning alone can't be the final answer. People can learn how to make bombs. That's not the purpose of life, is it?" Arnie is full of questions and ideas, the kind that many self-respecting church-goers would never ask a pastor, but they are often the kinds of questions that are going through people's minds. Wouldn't it be good for every pastor to have an Arnie or two with whom to stay real? This pastor does and has quoted and responded to Arnie's questions and ideas in sermons and on teaching occasions.

An important consideration for worship and preaching planning is how to get people to engage their daily life experiences in the "world out there" with the word of God. Sometimes a sermon addressing a current issue can be well introduced with a caring conversation. That is how Father Chip Stokes, Rector at St. Paul's Episcopal Church in Delray Beach, Florida, approached it when the Most Rev. Dr. Katharine Jefferts Schori became the twenty-sixth Presiding Bishop of the Episcopal Church, the first female presiding bishop in the history of the church. After her installation on November 4, 2006, Father Stokes gave a sermon on women in the church. His sermon began by having the people in the pews turn to one another and talk about a woman of faith who was important to them. He then debriefed the small group conversations by discussing some of the conversations with the larger worshiping community. Next, he integrated those comments into his sermon that reflected on women in the Bible and in the history of the church. It served not only to present a creative, stimulating, and somewhat extemporaneous homily, it also offered some much needed pastoral care to those who were not sure what to think about a female presiding bishop.

On another Sunday, following hurricane Wilma, which caused several hundred thousand dollars worth of damage to St. Paul's, including to the sanctuary, Fr. Chip Stokes began his sermon with a caring conversation. He asked the people in the pews to turn to one another in groups of four or five – children, youth adults, seniors – and share what Wilma had been like for them. Specifically, he encouraged them to communicate how they were feeling just before the storm hit, what it was like during the storm, and how they felt when it was all over. "We were all feeling shell-shocked. You could feel it in the air, and I wanted to give people a chance to talk about what they were feeling," Stokes said. There was incredible pastoral power in providing everyone, parents especially, an opportunity to share what they were feeling with their children in worship. We often try to shelter our children and not tell them what we are feeling, but often they know intuitively, and such an exercise gets the truth out on the table. This experience was cathartic for those who attended worship that morning; the large number of people who told Father Stokes afterwards how much they appreciated having the opportunity to talk about their experience of Wilma in worship confirmed the positive response.

Pastor Greg Kaufmann, who serves both as a regional and national leader in the Evangelical Lutheran Church in America, tells the story of attending worship at Riverside Baptist Church, where James Forbes was senior pastor. Kaufmann writes:

> It happened to be a Sunday when he gives over a portion of his preaching time (often 45 minutes!) to the members to talk with their neighbor about the theme of his sermon that day, and the text he was using. I happened to be sitting next to a woman who I later learned was his wife. We had only introduced ourselves by our first names! We talked passionately about what we thought the text was calling us to live out in our lives. She felt that the congregation needed to be more actively involved in the lives of mothers with young children throughout the week. I was equally passionate about connecting with the lives of teenagers once they affirmed their baptisms. Both of us promised to pray for each other and our sense of calling. We then listened to James Forbes preach. That sermon was heard with very different and finely tuned ears! This kind of worship and preaching that intentionally includes open conversations between worshippers is

memorable, significant in the lives of worshippers, and can happen in churches of different traditions.

"Where the preacher stands" can be a metaphor for larger issues of theology and ethics. For our purposes, it has concrete implications as a literal statement: where in the assembly of worshippers does the preacher stand? With attention to the dialogical nature of worship, it is fitting for a preacher, at least on occasion, to stand closer, more eye-to-eye with worshippers. However, there are some pastors for whom such a style simply doesn't work. In that case, using a manuscript in a pulpit or lectern may need to be the preferred location. But a sermon can still have that "dialogical" edge, no matter where the sermon is delivered. Keeping a spirit of conversation with the issues and questions of people's lives is important to the preaching of the church.

Worship and Preaching are Cross+generational

If we want Christian children and youth, then we need to surround them with Christian adults (the fifth of the Five Principles), people of faith who speak, model, and pray the faith. This principle requires that worship have a cross+generational dimension. There are elements of worship that speak to all generations on a deep level and join the generations in a dance of living faith. But even these demand that leaders be attentive to the convictions, questions, and experiences of all ages. For example, don't put small children in the back of the worship space where all they see are the backs of the people in front of them. Likewise, within the first minutes of a sermon, do or say something that attracts the attention of children and youth.

One mother reported that her daughter had done something unexpected the previous Sunday. The little girl usually gets a "busy bag" (a resource to keep younger children busy during the sermon) just as the sermon is starting. However, that Sunday the little girl did not get the bag. Instead, she stayed in her seat and listened to the sermon. The mother was surprised by this change of behavior and asked her why she was just sitting there and not getting her bag. The daughter responded,

"He's talking to me." The mother asked, "Who is?" The daughter said, "He is. The preacher. He usually talks to you. Today he is talking to me." The preacher was a guest preacher and did something that caught the attention of the child. He didn't preach from the pulpit; he stood in front of the worshipping community and as he spoke he made a lot of eye contact with the people seated in the rows in front of him.

There is no single way of capturing the attention of various generations, but on this particular Sunday a little girl saw a preacher at her level speak in a way that engaged her that day. Maybe he looked her in the eyes. Maybe she caught his glance. Perhaps it was just the change of routine, a different preacher standing in a different location. Perhaps it was that the preacher was standing close to her. Maybe it was his style of preaching that gave her the impression that what was happening now was a bit more conversational. Whatever it was that attracted her attention, she knew, "Today he is talking to me." What was happening that day was meant for her. Clearly, this reflects a cherished biblical image from the gospels. Shouldn't Jesus' emphasis on the centrality of children (see Matthew 19:13-15; Mark 10:13-16; Luke 18:15-17) have implications for public worship, and remind us that all children should be able to discern that what happens there is meant for them, too?

It is worth a preacher's awareness to explore ways that can reach out to different ages, especially the young. It is also important to acknowledge that while the little girl was captivated, someone else in the worship service could have been mumbling, "He needs to get back in the pulpit where he belongs, where he can be seen better!" Congregational leaders know there are no magic answers that will satisfy everyone. However, there is value in wanting to reach out to children during worship, including a sermon. That attitude presents a worship priority worth honoring.

One congregation has a tradition of having empty nesters sit next to families with young children. That congregation has found that this works well to help children focus on singing hymns and to eagerly await other portions of the worship service. Many of these empty nesters are identified as "Splash Families" to the children. *Splash* is a resource from Augsburg Fortress that connects non-relative adults with newly baptized children and their families.[6]

One simple and meaningful tradition incorporated by a congregation concludes the children's sermon with words from the congregation directed back to the children. The worshipping community says to the children, "You are a dearly loved child of God." The children respond back, "And so are you." What a simple yet touching way of connecting the generations in worship. So often having a children's sermon or some other kind of moment with children up front in worship becomes an endearing but passive experience for the larger worshipping community. Parents and grandparents strain their necks to get a good look at their children up front, perhaps getting a cute wave from a child. The pastor or some other leader offers a teaching moment for the children and the older worshippers smile and watch. But couldn't that moment capture something more, something that links the generations in a meaningful and memorable way? With the dialog just quoted, the youth and adults become more active participants in the life of these children. It may not be the last word in cross+generational contact, but it represents a step that models and promotes a larger cross+generational life of faith in worship. This congregation knows the dialog by heart and expects to be blessed by the exchange.

A Lutheran pastor prepared for Reformation Sunday one year using the Four Keys and with the larger Vibrant Faith Frame in mind. That Sunday was also Confirmation Sunday. The confirmands were asked to select a favorite Bible passage. In prior conversation with the pastor, the youth discussed their favorite passage and explained why it was a favorite passage. The confirmation youth recited their Bible passages on Reformation Sunday. They were encouraged to keep that text in their lives as part of their faith journeys and part of their growing devotional lives.

During the sermon, the pastor also named some Bible passages particularly meaningful to him. He concluded by encouraging the congregation to discuss passages that were especially meaningful to them with others over lunch that day. If they were alone for lunch or simply wanted to expand the conversation, the people were encouraged to call or email their children, grandchildren, or others significant to their lives and share their favorites with them.

The following week one couple told the pastor that they had done what he had asked them to do. They had emailed their grandchildren, but they also asked the grandchildren, in turn, to share their favorite Bible passages and why they were meaningful to them. Within an hour that Sunday afternoon, they had replies from all but two grandchildren. Before the evening ended, those last two had also responded.

Here is an example of a worship service that used a sermon to model the kind of cross+generational conversation people could have in their daily lives. As part of a sermon, the pastor reflected on meaningful conversations with young people. A devotional emphasis emerged through the sharing of favorite Bible passages. Grandparents served their grandchildren in the role of a spiritual elder. Perhaps a new family tradition could have started that day through an email request that connected the generations in faith.

The research from recent decades on factors in faith formation is quite clear: if we want Christian children and youth, we need to surround their lives with Christian adults, both family and non-family models of Christian faith.[7] Actively engaging young people in the life of the congregation and giving them leadership opportunities are tasks integral to lifelong faith formation as well.[8] I recently witnessed the installation of a pastor to a new congregational setting. The bishop spoke, the president of the congregation spoke, other congregational leaders spoke, and then a middle-school youth from the congregation addressed the new pastor as part of the installation ceremony. It was a perfect moment and a well-chosen example of how youth were both involved and leading in the congregation.

Sometimes young children are excellent readers and speakers. With encouragement and help with difficult words, their voices reading Scripture or offering prayers inspire all ages. One congregation takes the children out during the sermon to study Bible passages used in the worship service. They return before the end of the worship service with newly written prayers to be used during that very service, prayers that they themselves offer in front of the larger worshipping community. They are taught, they are equipped, and they help lead, all in the same worshipful and educational hour.

At one worship service, the assigned reader of a New Testament reading was not present. The congregation sat and waited for the reading, not knowing the reader wasn't even there. Eventually, Ben, a thirteen-year old youth got up from his seat, walked up to the lectern, found the reading to be read, and read the passage. After the service was over a couple of adults came up to him and thanked him for his fine reading, not knowing he was not the assigned reader. The youth laughed and said he simply noticed no one was walking to the lectern to read, so he did. The added laughter in this narrative is that his family did not realize he was not the assigned reader either. Without fanfare he simply took it upon himself to fill a need in the middle of worship. This is a youth and a congregation that knows how natural it can be to worship as a cross+generational community.

Numerous congregations give attention to children and youth through Milestones Ministries (explored more fully in chapter two—pages 37-44). There is a public worship component to many of these Milestone events. As part of the worship service, children and youth are recognized, blessed, and honored for their maturing lives and Christian faith. A congregation in Dilworth, Minnesota has nineteen different Milestone events that give focus to children and youth and their families. This means that on average, two to three times a month during the school year children and youth are leading portions of the worship service or being addressed and prayed for during worship. Pastor Mark Asleson notes that during these occasions, children and youth will lead the congregation in the Lord's Prayer, in reciting the Apostle's Creed, or helping with some other part of worship. At times, families also come forward and are blessed by the worshipping community.

That Minnesota congregation is gaining a reputation for being crazy about it children, youth, and families. Recently a woman from the congregation came up to the pastor to inform him that she was pregnant. She had previously been told that medically she could not have children. Now with tears in her eyes and with her face beaming she exclaimed, "Pastor Mark, now I can bring my child to Milestones." She has been blessing other children in worship. Now her child will get to be blessed, too!

Worship and Preaching are not Just Public Events: They Occur in the Home, Too

Or course worship is not just a public event. Households worship, too. It is often called "devotions" or "prayer time" or something else. No matter what the name, it constitutes the spiritual worship of the home. Most everything mentioned in this chapter has lifted up the vital partnership between the ministry of the congregation and the ministry of the home. Worship is a part of the life of the Christian home as well as the Christian congregation. There is a missional focus to the home and its reach into family relationships, friendship ties, the neighborhood, and community. Dialog is vital to healthy home life. And even if the home is the dwelling of only one adult, it is still a dwelling place to welcome in a wide range of ages for a healthy cross+generational experience.[9]

A way of life, missional outreach, dialog, cross+generational community, and the home are all examples of how the Vibrant Faith Frame influences public worship and preaching. All of them can happen in most any congregation. These stories that come from congregations witness to an understanding of the life of the church that helps people bring the worship life of the community into the daily life of Christians. From the outposts of the homes where Christians dwell day in and day out, the kingdom of God reaches out into the larger world with the care that only the gospel of Jesus Christ brings. Introducing the Vibrant Faith Frame to the ministry of worship and preaching can help that happen more regularly.

4
Youth and Family Ministry

For years Vibrant Faith Ministries has taught that youth and family ministry is really about congregational renewal. In other words, doing youth and family ministry is not simply about youth and their families. In the 1980s Vibrant Faith Ministries was established as The Youth & Family Institute because the research and the experience of the church at that time made it clear that congregations could not do effective youth ministry without connecting with the homes of the youth.[1] However, it was not long before The Youth & Family Institute realized that congregations could not do effective youth and family ministry without also affecting the life of the larger congregation. The kind of outreach and discipleship formation needed for effective youth and family ministry is the same kind of outreach and discipleship formation needed from entire congregations. And that is a gift.

To nurture children and youth in the Christian faith necessitates adults—parents and other mentors—able to walk alongside younger followers of Jesus. To have adults whom children and youth trust and who claim and live Christianity instead of some other creed is essential. As adults walk alongside children and youth the language they use, the behaviors they demonstrate, the priorities they set, the commitments they make, the networks they establish in the larger world, the lifestyle they exemplify, all contribute to an embodied faith in Christ where faith is caught through relationships and experiences as well as taught in more formal settings. Such a holistic understanding of life and faith is necessary to make disciples willing and able to enter into God's world as followers of Jesus. Having a youth group sponsored by a congregation is never enough for this kind of lived faith. What is needed is a focus on the renewal of the life of the entire congregation where adults as well as youth are continually being discipled into Christ. Hence, meaningful and effective youth and family ministry necessitates the renewal of the entire congregation's life so that all people—children, youth, and adults—are shaped by a life in Christ.

The Study of Exemplary Congregations in Youth Ministry (EYM) "discovered that it is the culture of the whole church that is most influential in nurturing youth of vital Christian faith. The genius of these churches seems best described as a systemic mix of theology, values, people, relationships, expectations, and activities."[2] Congregations considered capable in nurturing faith in its youth may not have much of a youth ministry program, let alone one that is described as "dynamic" or "inspiring large numbers of youth." What such congregations have is a clarity of purpose and mission that pervades their entire existence as communities of faith that serve children, youth, and adults of all ages and stages with the good news of Christ Jesus. What a concept!

Youth ministry has a different look when the youth are not isolated from the larger congregation. Here is a case in point from Father Chip Stokes, Rector at St. Paul's Episcopal Church in Delray Beach, Florida:

When St. Paul's Episcopal Church first sponsored a Vibrant Faith Congregational Training weekend, we held the congregational workshop on Saturday and "four dotted" it, meaning that four generations were present, each person wearing a different colored "dot" on his or her shirt according to their generational cohort. We established small groups in which to have "caring conversations." In one of these groups was a life-long member of St. Paul's, a white male in his sixties. He is an attorney specializing in estate planning. In this same group was a teenage girl, an immigrant from Trinidad, in the Caribbean. From the caring conversation that began during that weekend, the two became friends. She ended up doing an internship in his law office, finished high school, and is now enlisted in the Marine Corps and is stationed in Iraq. He keeps in touch with her and joins with the whole church in praying for her each week. Thanks to the caring conversations, a young woman who would have just been a name on the prayer list for him, one among several from the parish serving in Iraq, is now someone he knows as a person and cares about.

Granted, most people do not hear or read this story and think youth ministry, but the future of the church depends upon this very kind of imaginative understanding of congregational youth ministry. The fifth of the Five Principles articulates an essential ingredient to the future of youth ministry, an ingredient experienced in our narrative by a teen and a older man representing very different cultural experiences but both a blessing to the other: If we want Christian children and youth, we need Christian adults. Implied in this principle is that every Christian adult is a Christian "parent." Such youth ministry affects the lives not only of youth but of the people blessed to be in contact and in ministry with them. It is youth ministry that supports people as they move out into the larger world of work, of establishing one's own young adult life, and even of deployment in an overseas military assignment.

A second story

The North Carolina Synod of the Evangelical Lutheran Church in America has committed itself to the work of the Vibrant Faith Frame by promoting Vibrant Faith Conferences, by coaching congregations to be "teaching congregations," and by training synod staff. One of the synod strategies includes gathering congregational leaders to evaluate progress, tell stories of where the ministry is working, and explore issues that need attention. The group of about forty people included a group of middle school and high school youth. The youth raised the concern of wanting more contact with older adults in their congregation. The older adults in attendance responded with caution more than delight. They pointed out that they did not know how to talk the language of the youth. A senior high youth said, "That would seem a little phony if you did." A middle school youth added, "We want your stories. Where any of you in the war?" It was not clear what war was being asked about, but it was clear that the youth were interested in the unique life experiences of the older generations.

The North Carolina example was told to a group of middle schoolers, high schoolers, and adults during an education hour between worship services one Sunday morning in Fort Collins, Colorado. It piqued the curiosity of one man who was a parent of one of the youth present at the same event. He asked what the youth present would think if an adult from the congregation came up to them, called them by name, and started a conversation. As moderator of the conversations, I randomly picked out a youth and asked how he thought he would react to a conversation with an adult in the public and congregational setting. The youth responded that he would like that. The conversations that followed reinforced an openness to and desire for cross+generational conversations.

Between the education hour and the second worship service, I found myself in a number of conversations with youth and with youth and adults together as they continued to discuss the topic of more conversations between the generations. In one conversation I discovered that a youth I was talking to was the daughter of the man who raised the question about the comfort level of youth being in conversation with adults in the congregation. I asked that daughter if she was okay with her dad's question or if it made her feel uncomfortable. She responded that her dad's question was just fine with her. While she does not speak for all youth, her response does show the value of finding out what each particular youth is thinking and feeling, and it does show that youth are interested in conversations with older people.

These vignettes reflect recent research and other empirical evidence by Vibrant Faith Ministries regarding the lives of youth. Generally speaking, today's youth are open to and even eager for meaningful contact with adults. The adults, like parents, grandparents, and other mentors in the lives of youth, often are not aware of this desire or of how to respond. The data suggests the response is simple: be yourselves and tell us your stories of life, love, sacrifice, and faith. Then, listen to the youths' questions, issues, and passions. The youth want to explore God and relationships. Will the adult community of faith have the courage, interest, and passion to respond?

Not a New Approach, Just Not the Norm

These observations and recommendations for youth and family ministry are not really new, just not the norm for many congregations today. Phil, a retired pastor, heard about the Vibrant Faith Frame and immediately affirmed the approach from his own recollections of congregational life. As a college student in the 1950s, whenever Phil came home for Christmas each year, his pastor invited him to come down to his office. As a pastor himself later on, Phil never forgot the impact of those visits with his pastor and committed to find ways to reach out to the young people in his own pastoral ministry. Phil recalled what it felt like to have his pastor show interest in him. He felt the sense of value that "He wanted to talk to me."

That young college student later became Pastor Phil. He established for himself a clear objective to connect directly with young people. Before the concept of mentor was established in congregations, he put together what he called the "Friend and Faith" program, linking adults with youth. He began the program in 1969 with a three-to-four-week Bible study. After those weeks, adults and youth paired up to meet once a month for the rest of the school year. The pairs met in the church building and were given assignments. They would make three kinds of pastoral care visits during the year: to someone who had just lost a loved one, to someone who had been very sick, and to someone who had just joined the church. The pairs would then meet in small groups and discuss what they had experienced. Interesting stories came out of it that reminded youth and adults alike of the passion and meaningfulness of life and faith.

Pastor Phil was convinced that understanding the faith had less to do with knowledge and more to do with relationships. He was confident that it was through such relationships that youth would feel accepted in the worship community and that the Christian faith would become rooted in their lives. One goal of Friend and Faith was to ensure that young people in eighth and ninth grade would have someone who knew them when they came to worship, someone other than their own parents. As it turned out, after being paired, Pastor Phil realized that the youth got to know ten to fifteen other adults from the pairing—through the one adult's network of friends and family in the congregation and community. Pastor Phil observed that it changed the experience of being the church: "It's a real community; it is not an institution; it's live people."

In that first year of the Friend and Faith program, there was a youth that Pastor Phil described as a boy "you did not want in your confirmation class. He could cause a lot of trouble." As a result of the Friend and Faith partnership, the boy told Pastor Phil that it was the first time an adult had ever listened to him. The boy had been moved to tears by the experience.

Pastor Phil established a pattern of interviewing sophomores in high school just prior to confirmation and then again in their senior year. Phil was amazed by the consistent comments of both the sophomores and seniors: if it had not been for the Friend and Faith program that gave them an adult community of care and exposure to people's real life experiences and faith responses, many of the youth would have been at a job or doing athletics instead of being engaged in the life and ministry of the congregation.

Over the years Friends in Faith expanded in that congregation in ways that fit the Vibrant Faith Frame even more fully. With Pastor Nathaniel, a new associate pastor in the congregation, Pastor Phil encouraged the adult friends of youth to stay connected with their youth throughout their high school years, not ending at tenth grade confirmation as had been originally intended. Each non-relative adult could only have one youth partner – thereby connecting youth to far more adults in the congregation than if one adult could have multiple youth partners. After one's youth graduated from high school and headed off to work, college, war, or whatever, the adult became eligible to have a new friend in faith. Almost all re-upped! They loved it. So did the youth. Decades later, Pastor Nathaniel is still in touch with his friend in faith, now a Lieutenant Colonel in the US Air Force.

One man in another congregation learned about the openness of youth not by reading research, but by being a confirmation mentor. Here is his story:

> *[We] got together seven or eight times to discuss our respective faith journeys and talk about issues that we as Christians encounter in our daily walks. It was heartening to spend time with a young person who has a knowledge of the Bible and tries to live in a manner that is consistent with his faith. We often hear of concerns about today's young people and whether matters of faith are important to them. Jon serves as affirmation of many youths who do choose to follow the Lord's will.*

> *Jon was impressive in his comfort in conversing with an older adult whom he did not know. We engaged in many conversations that were active processes with participation from the both of us. His maturity in these discussions was impressive.*

> *I think it shows that people of all ages can find very important shared values when faith in the Lord is the common denominator.*

Although this mentor was biased by what people say about "today's young people and whether matters of faith are important to them," he learned otherwise. He also learned by experience that the youth was comfortable being in conversation with "an older adult whom he did not know." Some of the best learning we ever do is that which is learned by experience, especially when it breaks down former assumptions. An important ingredient to youth and family ministry is adults getting comfortable being and growing with youth.

The examples listed above can easily be written off as "anecdotal" except for the fact that these accounts are reinforced by three decades of research.[3] One of those studies sought to understand the experience of young people who remained in the life of the church after high school. The goal was to determine just what factors kept the youth involved. That study became a precursor to a much larger EYM Study reported in *The Spirit and Culture of Youth Ministry*. The initial study determined that the primary faith influence on the lives of youth was the degree to which faith was practiced in the home. A very close second factor was having three or more adults engaged in the youth's life of faith. Next came the influence of three or more months of service as a Christian practice. Fourth and fifth influences were based on being apprenticed into the leadership of the congregation and meaningful involvement in the life of the congregation. Number six was an excellent senior high and young adult ministry.[4]

When considering effective youth or youth and family ministry in a congregation, the influence of family and other adults has to be given primary attention. Family experiences and other adults in the lives of these young adults were at the top of researched youth's list, a finding consistent with the data that later came out of the EYM Study. However, when congregations panic and recognize that something is not working for their ministry with youth, one of the first ideas the leadership identifies is to work on a more active youth group. The alarm is rung to get some interested folk to invest time in youth, or, better yet, to hire a youth worker to bring in the kids. Insufficient attention is given to what happens once the youth are gathered together. The apparent objective is just to get the kids together in a safe space, off the streets. What is called for instead today is a larger vision of what youth and family ministry can look like, and how it can be more cross+generational and not exist as a youth group isolated from the larger congregation that meets at its own time, with its own leaders, and in its own space.

This all-too-typical model of youth ministry is another example of the Great Omission (the neglect of the role of the home in faith formation).[5] Instead of valuing and equipping parents and other adults to care for the youth in a cross+generational community, congregational leaders select a young, rather inexperienced, and often underpaid and untrained youth worker to do so. This model works neither for the faith formation of youth, nor for the wellbeing of the youth worker. Congregations are filled with stories of young adults who in good faith tried to make a difference, only to end up discouraged and often leaving the church in shame or disgust.

It is not that a youth group is unimportant, but it is number six in the list of faith factors identified above. If congregations want that more active youth ministry that lasts, then congregations need to pay attention to faith factors number one through five and also seven and eight (Christian peers and help during personal crisis) as part of a larger, more broadly based and organic youth ministry program. If a youth worker is hired to build up the youth ministry, then his or her job is not simply to get the youth together for a hay ride, bowling night, or even a worship service. That youth worker also has to equip the homes of the youth with Christian faith practices, engage the youth with other caring and faithful Christian adults, give them meaningful service activities as part of Christian vocation, and enable their participation in the larger life of the congregation, including by giving them a significant role in the leadership of the congregation.

Creating a Different Scorecard to Evaluate a Successful Youth Ministry

For most congregations and their leaders, a successful youth ministry continues to be a valued goal. However, that requires much more than a room filled with energetic youth. A better way to measure a successful youth ministry is by determining how many of the youth are still engaged with the life and work of the church years after youth ministry is over. Youth ministry that has scores of youth involved in a youth group but never seen again in the life of the church after high school stretches the notion of what "successful" youth ministry means. One congregation has a very "successful" Sunday evening youth worship service that routinely brings in five hundred youth. The congregation's leadership is considering dropping the service because they are not seeing that ministry effort resulting in lasting effects. The kids are gone after high school.

But need it be an either/or proposition? Instead of abandoning a worship service that obviously attracts many youth, what if the congregation made the worship more cross+generational and fostered faith practices that connected the youth with their homes and the care and involvement of other mentors? What if the youth made commitments to a number of mission trip[6] options that included adults of various ages so that the generations could learn from each other and be nurtured in the Christian faith together? What if adults helped lead the youth service with youth, just like congregations want children and youth to help lead other worship experiences? What if the youth helped with children's Milestones Ministry events, and children and adults participated in youth's milestones like a first driver's license, mission trip, or graduation? What if we chose a scorecard for youth ministry that aimed at lifelong faith formation and the factors that facilitate it instead of large numbers of energetic kids in a room for three or four years?

From Swedish Meatballs to Youth and Family Ministry

Many congregations have revered traditions that bring members together for some kind of fellowship activity. Usually, that activity is the possession of the adults, often the older adults. For over fifty years one congregation with a Swedish heritage had held a combined St. Lucia and Advent Vespers celebration. The choirs provided beautiful music, and Scripture was read along with the story of St. Lucia. One young woman from the congregation was always asked to serve as St. Lucia and lead everyone to the fellowship hall for Swedish treats. More "seasoned" members of the congregation made Swedish Meatballs, rice pudding, herring, cucumber rye sandwiches, sandbuckles, and a variety of other treats. Those over fifty attended the event; the one girl serving as St. Lucia was the only child there.

The transformation happened when the Vibrant Faith Frame was incorporated into the festivities. The church hired a youth and family director who had a degree in youth and family ministry from Augsburg College, a college program that had trained this graduate in the Vibrant Faith Frame. She stepped in and tweaked the existing annual Swedish Meatball Dinner. Because of the dwindling numbers of people who attended the event, the sponsors of the dinner were willing to consider some changes. It was intentionally made cross+generational. Families with children were asked to come and make the food with the older members so the children and families could learn about the Swedish heritage of the church. The children now help serve the food, and they attend the Advent event. Rather than having pews filled with white- and gray-haired folk, the pews are now filled with families of all configurations and there is an energy at the Advent Vespers that only children can bring. The annual Swedish Meatball Dinner and Advent Vespers became transformed into a time to nurture relationships, talk about the faith of today's generations as well as generations past, and delight in the joy of serving others in a community of faith.

Another congregation changed the dynamics of the congregation's spring-cleaning, something that had primarily involved the retired men in the congregation. Recognizing that the home is church, too, the homes of shut-ins were added to the list of property to be cared for during the spring-cleaning weekend. The leadership also sought to bring together various generations to work in the congregation and in the homes of shut-ins. One elderly woman was so touched by the two fourteen-year olds who came and helped her clean her home that she asked if they could stay and visit with her instead of going on to the next home. The leadership wisely discerned the advantage of letting those two teens bless and be blessed by an elder in the faith that Saturday afternoon.

Yet another congregation has a cross-generational Hanging of the Greens during the third week of Advent. Members decorate the sanctuary, including the Christmas trees in the sanctuary and fellowship hall. Children help in all cases and are in charge of at least one of the trees. Participants share family Advent traditions, enjoy a meal, have a devotional, and then go home. They have successfully Four Keyed the decorating of the church, and it is done cross+generationally.

Connecting with Youth

The Vibrant Faith Frame enriches youth ministry and expands it to include families, other adults, and a whole host of other key factors in the life of the congregation, factors that affect the faith life of children and youth. It need not be a conflict between traditional youth ministry activities and Vibrant Faith Frame youth and family ministry. Unfortunately, some have been known to teach a youth and family ministry model in a way that suggests youth ministry is no longer needed. The thinking goes that congregations just need to pay attention to families and meaningful contact for youth with AAA adults. However, there is a place for both the age-focused ministry with youth as well as the ministry that connects youth with broader, multi-generational experiences. Vibrant Faith Ministries itself promotes Peer Ministry, a teen-caring-for-teen Christian formation model that serves as a cornerstone to congregational youth ministry. Peer Ministry creates a caring and welcoming atmosphere that better enables teens to connect faith and daily life with special attention to how teens can care for and serve other teens, especially during times of critical need.[7]

A foundational premise of Peer Ministry states, "You are not doing youth ministry until youth are doing ministry." The critical contribution of Peer Ministry is its emphasis on the Christian faith of youth and on encouraging and equipping youth to be actively engaged in ministry, not standing on the sidelines being entertained for a few years. As one young adult said about his youth ministry experience, "My involvement in the church as a child and teenager had been largely social, and I found other outlets for that as a young adult."[8] Youth ministry that is social, entertainment ministry primarily geared to keeping kids off the streets and "safe" is not a sustainable or valuable understanding of youth or youth and family ministry.

This same observation can be made about adult ministries. The "attractional model" of ministry that seeks to bring people into a comfortable religious setting in the congregation is not enough to fulfill the call of being the church and making disciples. Whether it is youth ministry or any form of child or adult ministry, the discipleship model that promotes missional outreach represents the only viable model for the life and work of the church. Again, this illustrates how youth and family ministry involves the renewal of the larger congregation and not simply a youth program.

Youth ministry worthy of its name involves a number of options like experiential Bible studies, relational youth ministry that includes creative and enjoyable activities, various types of small group ministry, and meaningful service activities including mission trips. These are all examples of youth ministry that can be enriched through Peer Ministry because Peer Ministry lives out the Vibrant Faith Frame, connecting the youth with the Six Places of Ministry, that larger arena of the church that takes Christians far beyond the walls of a church building. Through it, youth become wedded to a Christian life and faith that links children and youth to homes, to congregation, to community, to culture, and to creation. In other words, Peer Ministry promotes a "for-God-so-loved-the-world" Christian faith instead of a "me-and-Jesus" affair. The traditional understanding of a "youth group" involves youth activities that turn the youth inward on themselves. The "youth ministry" of Peer Ministry promotes activities and relationships that face outward, to the world God loves and calls us to serve. The Five Principles are themselves relationally driven and lived out in Peer Ministry in many ways, including the home life of peer ministers. Many parents of peer ministers have asked their congregations, "What have you done to my son/daughter?" These parents love the results. A youth trained in caring relationship skills ends up affecting his or her home life. The Four Keys are foundational practices in Peer Ministry and the outcome is a AAA disciple who happens to be under the age of twenty-one. In the both/and world of youth and family ministry, the Vibrant Faith Frame promotes youth ministry that is more than teens being with teens, and more than connecting youth with their parents. The Vibrant Faith Frame promotes youth doing ministry to all the world (the Six Places of Ministry), among all the generations (the Five Principles), through a Christian spirituality of faith practices (the Four Keys), and with the result of nurturing AAA youth and AAA adults. These elements of church life are not new, of course, just in tension with the attractional model of congregational life that looks inward to self and local church only instead of outward to the world that is God's.

The Vibrant Faith Frame identifies components for renewing the larger church as well as youth ministry. It gets at the heart of congregational renewal. Effective youth and family ministry cannot happen without the renewing of the life of the congregation, not just families. It connects youth with the other generations, not just the generations in one's own family because the Christian faith is not nurtured in isolated homes. Youth and family ministry renews the faith journey of all the generations, as all the generations are needed to walk with and do ministry with youth.

Let's not Wait until the Children are Youth to do Youth Ministry

Instead of dividing congregational ministries into distinct and age-segregated tasks, we do well to promote closer work between ages and ministry teams. A prime example is the areas of children and youth ministries in a congregation. Children's ministry serves as a critical recruitment tool for youth ministry, and if a congregation wants to have an effective youth ministry, it also needs to have an effective children's ministry.

Often children's ministry is an extension of Sunday school and perhaps vacation Bible school. That can work well as long as parents and other adults are actively engaged with the children. *Together in Faith*[9] is an example of a family-based faith formation program (for some congregations it serves as a wonderful pre-confirmation program) for children ages three through grade five. It involves parents and other adults and brings the faith journey back into the homes following the educational sessions. This model of children's ministry bonds children and parents together and joins household to household. By the time the children enter the stage for youth ministry or confirmation class, an attitude and expectation of involvement has had years to develop. Fewer children and adults are lost in that process, and a more robust youth ministry has already begun because the youth and their parents are actually present and waiting for more.

Other congregational curriculums are taking advantage of the critical link between children and home. Young families are being connected with sponsor individuals and families who actively support and engage these young families with faith-formative care, usually through some form of the Four Keys. Congregational meals, training sessions, and resources combine to serve young families with human and curricular resources that make it clear that children and their families are not to be ignored or forgotten as people grow in the grace of God over time.

Learn Their Names!

For years Vibrant Faith Ministries (and its predecessor The Youth & Family Institute or TYFI) has been presenting a more effective approach to youth and family ministry. One of the strategies that gets both a chuckle and a lot of heads nodding in agreement is the directive to learn the names of the youth in the congregation. How can our congregations do the relational, faith-nurturing ministry with youth and adults working together without even knowing the youth by name? Of course such a cross+generational ministry means more than knowing a name, but it is a good place to begin.

> ❝ Learn the names of the youth
> in the congregation. ❞

Dick Hardel, former executive director of TYFI (now VFM) tells the story of his experience as pastor in a congregation in Florida. At one council meeting he projected pictures of all the seventh graders. It was a large congregation and there were scores of seventh graders. He asked that the council members call out the names of the youth as they appeared on the screen. About the only youth that were named were the ones who were children of council members. It was a rather dramatic way of pointing out that we do not know our own youth, not even their names.

How many adults would return to a congregation week after week if no one but their family members and closest friends called them by name? Probably not many. Why should we imagine that our youth feel like coming back week after week when nobody from the congregation calls them by name either?

One of the more effective methods of engaging adults with youth has been to ask governing boards to learn one or two or three youth by name and then to learn something about their lives, what makes them tick and gives them joy. All of a sudden, these adult leaders are engaging in youth and family ministry that lives out the Five Principles, begins to touch on the Four Keys, and results in AAA adults. Again, it's not rocket science, just the Vibrant Faith Frame that can change lives.

One congregation has a governing board of six members, one of whom is a high school youth. She has made it clear at those meetings that the way she has been greeted and cared for week after week has made a big difference in her interest in church and the Christian faith. The director for the Rotation Sunday School program is going to have the young council member go with her and talk to the Sunday school teachers, people who teach a three-week session and then are replaced by another rotation team. The director wants these teachers to hear through this girl's testimony how adults' ongoing care of children affects them. The director wants to encourage the short-term teaching teams to intentionally stay connected with the children even after they have finished teaching them. It means remembering names and stories and taking the time to connect with these children and youth over the years. This simple strategy and mindset is a cornerstone to a valuable youth ministry.

Here is one of those stories from a congregational member who had a cross+generational Christian education experience at a Vibrant Faith Congregational Training weekend. He describes his own experience with the VFM trainer who led the congregational experience:

[After a brief history of his faith journey, including a divorce and distancing himself from the church for awhile] God sent yet another messenger to further define my mission. Enter [the VFM trainer].

In the short time you spent with us this weekend, my commitment and passion has been further defined. Trust me when I tell you that after 28 years as a police officer, cynicism becomes an integral part of one's being. The LAST thing that I wanted to do was deal with kids. I raised two of my own, a son and a daughter. . . Jodi [his wife] serves as a confirmation guide, and I have been asked several times to do the same. Needless to say, I have not answered the call, thinking that I have nothing to contribute, nothing meaningful to say to someone of that age.

This morning [at a cross+generational experience], I found that, as usual, I was wrong. The time spent with our youth this morning was an epiphany. Not only did I see them reach out in our game, but in the small group discussions, I found that I actually did have something to contribute, and they in fact wanted to hear what I had to say.

I'm looking forward to becoming more involved with these wonderful young people and plan on at least volunteering for the mentor program, if not jumping in with both feet as a confirmation guide.

My wife and I have also engaged in meaningful conversation since yesterday on levels that we've not approached before. It's difficult to explain, but I feel a difference in our relationship that was not present three days ago as we have discussed our walk with Christ on a deeper level than we previously have.

Thank you so very much, and add me to the list of people whose lives you have profoundly touched. I'm sure the list is long.

May God bless you and your continuing work.

His pastor wrote the following message about that weekend:

It has already been fun to see how "cross generational" ideas are developing. We are beginning to have a greater appreciation for the gifts that people of all ages provide in a ...culture that tends to segregate people by age categories. This is a foundation building discipleship effort!

These comments help identify youth and family ministry that is more about congregational renewal and lifelong faith formation than about parents and their kids showing up for a few years during middle school and high school. A retired police officer realizes he has something to contribute to the life and faith of youth, and the youth want what he has to offer. This man's marriage also benefited from the Vibrant Faith Frame even though he did not come to the congregational training for marriage and faith enrichment. The pastor and the lay leader both celebrate the power of cross+generational life and ministry and the pastor names it correctly as discipleship, not youth ministry. It is a ministry that brings together the God-given gifts of all God's children to nurture faith in a cross+generational community.

Youth and family ministry grounded in the Vibrant Faith Frame offers a very different set of goals and values from the attractional youth ministry model of the twentieth century that isolated youth from the rest of the congregation. No wonder those youth exited the larger congregational life after high school. They were never part of that larger congregational life to begin with.

One congregation embraced the both/and thinking of youth and family ministry when it built its youth room for youth ministry. The congregation put the youth room in the middle of the administrative office suite, right in the middle of all the action. This congregation wants to see its youth. This congregation wants to interact with its youth. And this congregation wants the youth to be at the heart of life of the congregation and its choices for a vibrant faith for children, youth, and adults.

Some Other Ideas for a Vibrant Faith Youth Ministry Focus

Youth and family ministry touches all areas of the life of the congregation. It no longer represents an isolated age group. Faith formation of children and youth with a community of AAA adults around them can have a rich and varied look that includes the following:

- Any gathering for children, youth, and adults that practice the Four Keys
- Any gathering of caring adults to nurture adult faith with an eye to reaching out to children and youth to equip them with a vibrant faith
- Training adults in discipleship and outreach before many of those adults become parents (why wait?)
- Doing Milestones Ministry, beginning with dedication or baptism and continuing throughout the ages and stages of life
- Worship that communicates an awareness of the gifts, presence, and issues of children and youth and the adults around them
- Mission trips and other servant events that practice the Four Keys cross+generationally, preferably at least one adult for each youth in attendance
- High school youth trained and used as confirmation guides or middle school mentors

- Peer Ministry training that equips youth for caring conversations, devotional life, service, and faith-based rituals and traditions for use in home, congregation, community (especially schools), culture, and creation
- Youth studying sermon texts with pastor and other worship leaders to explore topics, questions, and issues that youth and others want to see named and addressed in sermons and the larger worship service
- Servant leadership at before school and after school programs for children and youth
- Adults intentionally mentoring youth

How we send our children, youth, and adults into the world as disciples of Christ is foundational to all efforts to nurture the Christian faith in children, youth, and adults. Vibrant Faith Ministries has built this foundation through the Vibrant Faith Frame for the renewal of the church.

5

STEWARDSHIP

I had been invited to sit down at a coffee shop to have a conversation with two fundraisers who work with the church on a national level. The conversation was initiated by one of them and joined by the second. The first wanted to make it clear how true it is that the home is church, too. This individual wanted Vibrant Faith Ministries to know that "fundraisers know that the church is in the home"—and specifically at the kitchen table. That is where he has experienced some of the deepest conversations and most heartfelt confessions of faith. There, in their homes at the kitchen table people disclose the passion of their faith and their desires for the work of the church to continue with their financial gifts.

The second fundraiser, a former parish pastor, concurred. He acknowledged that some of the most spiritual moments he has ever had in ministry were with people in their homes confessing their faith, their hopes, dreams, and concerns as they contemplated handing over large portions of their treasure for the work of God. It is in the home that people acknowledge that everything they have is a gift from God, a gift that now needs to be redistributed well for the glory of God and the needs of church and world.

Both fundraisers made it clear from their experience and observations that significant financial gifts do not often happen at congregational meetings. The level of contribution, commitment, and passion just does not happen as often in those public church settings as it does in the more intimate, more candid, and more vulnerable setting of one's own home, especially, it seems, at one's own table. These two church leaders agreed that not only are large sums of money committed to the work of the church at kitchen tables, it is also at their kitchen tables that faithful people express themselves as in no other setting with deep prayer, gratitude, commitment, and, sometimes, tears.

The danger of this initial example is that it can seem to endorse the standard views that stewardship is really about money. The truth is that the reverse is the case. One's financial choices and commitments exist as a direct expression of one's deepest core values, convictions, and faith. It parallels the adage, "Stewardship is everything I do after I say, 'I believe.'" As Jesus said, "For where our treasure is, there your heart will be also" (Matthew 6:21). Biblically, the concept of "heart" does not equate simply with emotion. The heart identifies the whole of the person's self, the mind, the will to act, as well as one's emotions. The heart represents the totality of one's life, including experiences that contribute to what one believes and how one uses one's treasure.

Those experiences that guide what a Christian believes in large measure emerge from the faith-forming work of the home in partnership with the faith-forming experiences that take place in the congregation. This is the case for children, for youth, and for adults of all ages. It is not that home and congregation are the only settings; they are simply the primary settings through which the church has a vested interest in blessing, equipping, and serving so that the word of God and the work of God may take place in a multitude of other settings.

Grace Lutheran in Hendersonville, NC gives us an example of that vital partnership of home and congregation in stewardship. A communal sense of stewardships develops through this strategic partnership. The congregation offers an after school program for students. It involves adults helping students with homework and engaging the students with time and conversation, Bible reading and prayer. Pastor Williams asked the study buddies, the adult participants in the program, to reflect on their experience and evaluate its usefulness (see pp. 147–50 in "Preschool and After School Programs" for the notes written by study buddy partners).

The responses were overwhelmingly positive. One study buddy, Betsy, a retired school teacher, talked about making a "new best friend" and growing spiritually with her study buddy. Betsy's commitment to Sandi's life was significant. And the commitment of the young girl and her mother was equally deep. Betsy's stewardship of talents and time as well as finances to do such things as travel to be with Sandi and to provide materials for science experiments made a difference in both their lives. It undoubtedly made a difference in more than just those two (consider the impact on the family and friends of both Sandi and Betsy). The study buddy comes to the after school program with an abundance of skills as a retired teacher. She has made a choice to use her own time on behalf of others. This is the larger world of Christian stewardship, living as a recipient of God's undeserved kindness and in some small measure loving the world that God loves as a reflection of God's perfect love for us. Christian stewardship leads to significant gains for people, in this case a "new best friend" and spiritual growth.

In 1 Corinthians 4:1 Paul refers to this way of life as being "servants of Christ and stewards of God's mysteries." As those who are entrusted with the mysteries of God's amazing grace and mercy, we become the servants of Christ and servants of those for whom Christ died. It changes everything we see. Being stewards of the mysteries of God leads us to do things to express that divine love in human relationships. One such example comes from Betsy and her study buddy, another comes from a member of another congregation using the Vibrant Faith Frame,

Morning Star Lutheran Church in Matthews, NC. The pastors asked for examples of how the Vibrant Faith Frame is being lived in daily lives. One person wrote the following story.

> *I have enjoyed learning about the Four Keys and when my mom came for a visit, I couldn't wait to share them with her. During her visit we tried to use them all, prayer before meals, service projects and conversations, but my favorite moment, strangely enough, was when she was leaving. We did the "Blessing for Those Traveling" from the book* For Everything A Season: 75 Blessings for Daily Life. *Since my mom doesn't speak English, I translated it into Finnish. My daughter Emily helped with prayers, and as a ritual we made a sign of the cross on Mom's forehead while saying: "Remember, God goes with you." I must confess, it was a little difficult to understand me through the sobbing and the tears, but it meant a lot to all of us. When Mom got home she called and said she had arrived safely and she felt it was because of the blessing.*

What a special moment. The beauty of living with the mysteries of God cannot be fully grasped ever in this life. The mysteries can, however, be given our attention and imagination through prayers, conversations, service projects, and a never-before-used blessing of a mother returning home to Finland. Sometimes the gestures and the efforts speak more powerfully when hard to understand through "the sobbing and the tears." This is the stewardship that shapes people's lives, their decisions, their use of time, the use of their spiritual gifts, and their use of the funds they have to support passions, causes, and creeds.

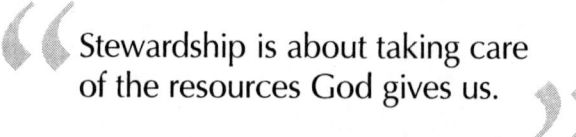

Stewardship is about taking care of the resources God gives us.

Stewardship is about protecting and using something that does not belong to those who use it. God directs us to use time, gifts, and possessions for good, not evil, for the greater good, not for selfish desires, for that which brings joy and delight, not that which sours and decays. Stewardship is about taking care of the resources God gives us, not about grabbing so much manna in the wilderness that it goes moldy before we can use it (Exodus 16:20).

To speak of being stewards of God's riches is to stand in direct opposition to the cultural assumption that we are self made (expressed as "I'm a self-made man/woman") and therefore entitled to all we acquire. Learning to become such stewards takes much more than a once-a-year fall stewardship drive to see what we can afford as a congregation next year. It takes understanding that stewardship is synonymous with discipleship, and that means following Jesus over one's entire lifetime. Such dedicated discipleship embodies a life of gratitude not demand, of humility not pride, of joy in the little things not needing more and more and bigger and bigger to feel happy.

Pastor Russ Sorensen of Bethany Lutheran in Rice Lake, Wisconsin approached his congregation's fall stewardship drive with this larger picture of Christian discipleship in mind. He led twenty-five Bethany Friendship Events that brought together four hundred members of the congregation in small groups that met in homes and in the church building. Pastor Sorensen stated that the purpose of the meetings "was to build relationships with Christ and with each other in the body of Christ." The people came together in small groups and discussed what it means to live as the body of Christ in the larger world. Notes Pastor Sorensen, "[O]ur response to God's blessings through the stewardship of life naturally came into the conversations." The Bethany Friendship Events were intentionally Four Keyed to model what the life of faith could look like in their own homes. He encouraged the people to invite others into their homes as an important part of Christian stewardship and hospitality. He showed them how easily this home hospitality could be done by using a congregational resource that gives numerous examples of how to use the Four Keys alone and with others.[1] Sorensen concludes, "With the very positive reaction to these events, we are even more encouraged to find ways to deepen our relationships with Christ and each other with cross-generational opportunities and meetings in homes." The Bethany Friendship Events are an example of approaching stewardship more as an ongoing expression of discipleship than as a one-time fund drive.

The Stewardship of Justice, Kindness, and Humility

Stewardship as discipleship is about the love of God and the love of neighbor (Matthew 22: 37-39). The worship of God through the care of others is a repeated premise of the Christian life. Micah answers the question of how to worship God: "He has told you, O mortal, what is good; and what does the LORD require of you but to do justice, and to love kindness, and to walk humbly with your God?" (6:8). Other prophets give a similar message (see Isaiah 1:10-17; Joel 2:12-13; Amos 5:21-24). James offers a similar description of the life of faith: "Religion that is pure and undefiled before God, the Father, is this: to care for orphans and widows in their distress, and to keep oneself unstained by the world" (1:27). To be a biblical and Christian steward is to reflect the love of God and neighbor. How we use our resources to support a local congregation is part of this, but it is not the whole meaning of Christian stewardship, not even close!

Christian stewardship promotes a life of abundance and not scarcity. God is not a miser. God fills all of life with what we need to live and thrive. God creates and distributes abundantly, and so, as the Apostle Paul notes in 1 Corinthians, "[We] are not lacking in any spiritual gift as [we] wait for the revealing of our Lord Jesus Christ" (1:7). Unfortunately, we do not distribute so well and consequently many around the globe go hungry despite God's abundance. The Six Locations of Ministry identify the personal and also universal reach of discipleship, including Christian stewardship.

One of those locations of ministry is creation. Christian stewards cannot stand on the sidelines of care for the earth when the Pentagon reports on the national security threat posed by climate change;[2] when approximately 16,000 children die each day from hunger-related problems;[3] and when 3.5 million people die each year from water-related diseases.[4] Our task is to share creation's life-giving resources.[5]

> " **To care for creation is to care for one's neighbor.** "

Some might say we should care primarily about spiritual things like following Christ and saving souls. Yet biblical spirituality does not separate the care of people's souls from the care of people's daily existence. Separating the spiritual world from the material world is key to Greek philosophy, but not to biblical theology. The Apostle Paul had to address this in 1 Corinthians 15 by pointing out—contrary to Greek philosophy—the importance of the resurrection of the body, not just the resurrection of some disembodied soul. Because of the devaluation of things of the earth, of physical matter, some didn't believe that Jesus really lived in the flesh. 1 John states that "every spirit that confesses that Jesus Christ has come in the flesh is from God" (4:2). Matter matters. Precisely because of that, John's letter raises the question, "How does God's love abide in anyone who has the world's goods and sees a brother or sister in need and yet refuses to help? (3:17). James addresses this directly as a matter of faith itself: "If a brother or sister is naked and lacks daily food, and one of you says to them, 'Go in peace; keep warm and eat your fill,' and yet you do not supply their bodily needs, what is the good of that? So faith by itself, if it has no works, is dead" (2:15-17). Biblical stewardship is quite serious about the needs of people for food, warmth, and shelter. For us in the twenty-first century, such care for others includes safeguarding creation so that sufficient water is available to drink and to nourish crops and sufficient food is available for all to consume.

> " **Matter matters.** "

Spiritual Gifts in the Body of Christ

Similarly, God distributes spiritual gifts for the body of Christ to do God's saving work in the world. One's spiritual gifts are not for maintaining and promoting the congregational campus but for serving the kingdom of God wherever one's life is situated, including home, congregation, neighborhood, work, and larger world. This stands in contrast to those spiritual gifts inventories that look at people's abilities as ways to respond to congregational needs. In fact, spiritual gifts are to be used to care for the world that God so loves (John 3:16) ... as well as to maintain vibrant congregations. Too often congregations use spiritual gift inventories or time and talent sheets in a way that ignores God's call to serve one's neighbor wherever that neighbor is in the world. Christian stewardship is how we live out our Christian vocation, our Christian calling in the world. Inventories like Strength Finder and Dependable Strengths address the larger view that assesses one's whole life and how to respond to one's gifts, passions, and personality to serve the neighbor.[6]

Stewardship leadership in a congregation has the important task of helping people name and refine their gifts so that they may faithfully praise, serve, and love God and God's world. Most congregations give the vast majority of their attention to the needs of congregational services and budgets. Stewardship at home, at work, at school, and in the community and larger world is also an important aspect of Christian vocation.

Four Ways to Emphasize Vibrant Faith Stewardship

There are four implications of spiritual gifts in the body of Christ that we often overlook. First, no one individual has all the gifts. Faith that is formed through relationships is meant to be relational in its execution of love of God and neighbor. Most every assignment and position in the congregation requires gifts not entirely contained within any one person. Stewardship is a communal activity, not a private affair. One person may have the vision and leadership skills needed, but not the organizational ability to work out details. Another person may have many gifts required to accomplish an important ministry task but not be a good communicator. However, the body of Christ does have the requisite gifts. It is the "body" of Christ. We are stewards together, as a team. Often congregations get frustrated with the gifts a particular person (including paid church staff) does not have instead of celebrating the gifts they do have and looking to other people for the missing gifts. No one has all the needed gifts, talents, skills, and passions to do all work equally well. Where there are gaps, let them be filled by people who demonstrate them and are recognized for them by others in the congregation. Many a youth and family director is great with ideas, vision, and relationships but not so keen on details. Instead of humiliating that person for gifts not theirs, a sound stewardship ministry in the congregation prayerfully and prudently goes about discovering where those other gifts are in the lives of other people. That is stewardship filled with grace and mercy instead of law and judgment!

> We are stewards together, as a team.

Second, since the home is church, too, instead of congregational stewardship focusing on one budget (the congregation's annual budget), effective and faithful stewardship acknowledges that there are numerous budgets that can come to the aid of vital ministry. If a congregation has 125 households or home churches, then the congregation has 126 annual budgets with which to carry out meaningful ministry. After a congregation's budget has been approved, many creative ideas for ministry can still surface, for God's work is not limited to a budget approval at an annual meeting. When people hear the word "budget," too often the focus of the thinking and conversation becomes how to make sure the money holds out until the end of the budget year instead of seeing the money as a tool with which to serve God's mission. When new ideas to serve God's mission do surface, if the congregation's budget cannot locate the dollars, then there are 125 other budgets that just might. It is amazing how much ministry can get done once those other budgets are lifted up for what they are: God's! God's people are energized by God's call to love, serve, and obey. When there is clear need and prayerful discernment that something is God's call to God's people, dollars flow. When ministry is limited to what was approved eight months ago, dollars stop flowing, and the attention turns to remaining solvent until the end of the fiscal year.

This very concept was part of a congregational leadership meeting one Sunday afternoon. A new idea emerged that was received with great enthusiasm by those present. The people present wanted to build FaithChests® to bolster a Milestones Ministry emphasis that would also serve as outreach to people not part of the congregation. The leaders also chuckled that it just wasn't in the congregation's budget. All of a sudden $20 bills started appearing on the table (money from people's home budgets). Before long, the cash was in hand to start a new ministry not conceived nine months prior to that day. And the leaders left laughing and smiling and hopeful. Nearly a year later those leaders were still laughing and telling the story of freedom for ministry beyond one budget's capabilities. They also gave thanks to God that many FaithChests® had been built and children and family's lives had been touched by that form of outreach and Christian faith formation.

A third implication is Christian vocation that addresses how one's gifts of time, treasure, and talent get named and claimed for the kingdom of God through the church in the home. That home may be of a single adult or several young adult friends sharing housing. It may be of a widow, widower, or a couple of grandparents. It may be a single parent home or a home with two parents and one or more children, some living at home, some on their own. All are stewards of God's grace who live with joy and thanksgiving for what God has given them to share with others: good news of Jesus Christ and the life of the kingdom of God that he brings right now. A congregational stewardship drive that does not highlight this larger sense of church in the world through an exploration of Christian vocation is missing most of its calling as a stewardship emphasis in the congregation. Let's not forget the profound discipleship and stewardship that takes place at a kitchen table or in a backyard.

A fourth implication for a congregation's stewardship emphasis is also contained in the principle that the home is church. One congregation had conceived a major addition to its current facilities. There was great excitement around the need for more worship and fellowship space. But when all the costs were added up, the price tag was just too much. It would have required a doubling of current weekly offerings. The plan was postponed.

Quickly a spirit of discouragement arose among the leaders: so much promise not to be realized. The senior pastor recognized the negative climate that resulted from the postponement of the building expansion and rose to the occasion. The cost of sanctuary construction had initially been projected at $4.2 million. He writes:

> *As discouraging as that was, our VFM coach reminded us of the wealth God had already provided in each member's home. With 225 households there was a greater church facility resource than we could ever imagine let alone ever construct. The coach encouraged council members to invite people into their homes for caring conversations, meals, and devotions. They in turn reminded members of the congregation that God's house is wherever God's people are – so don't overlook where you dwell. Members have been asked to share faith stories of what was happening in their church house (their home). Their sharing of moments of serving, traditions enjoyed, devotions held and even daily conversations were inspirational. This is the real church 24/7 and not just church on the Sabbath. As a result [of reminding ourselves of this], members were praying for one another, faith was being shared, devotion was deepened, commitments were strengthened, the joy of giving and sacrificing multiplied that later resulted in an overwhelming response for a new sanctuary to be constructed. But even if a new sanctuary were never to be constructed, what happened during that time continues even today: the home becomes Holy, set apart for God's glory.*

Thanks be to God for the stewardship of the larger church.

Living as Stewards of the Mysteries of God with the Four Keys

Stewards of God's benevolence live in this world as people whose life and faith has been shaped by trusted relationships in the home, congregation, and larger social settings. As such, it is important to speak, reflect, and live a life that communicates gratitude and generosity for all that God does and all that we receive. That happens most effectively through the four foundational practices called the Four Keys. The chapter concludes with the following examples to consider and customize for use in one's own congregation and church in the home:

Caring Conversations

- In your conversations with others, listen closely to the important issues, core values, passions, faith, and doubt expressed
- Tell others about the gifts you see in their lives. We seldom grasp our own gifts to be used for others. Stewardship of gifts is a communal project
- Discuss with others how to use your resources wisely, faithfully, and joyfully
- Look up the following words in a dictionary and discuss how these terms connect with each other for Christians: steward/ stewardship, discipleship, vocation
- Identify times to talk with friends and/or family about how you want to spend time, money, and the use of your abilities with gratitude to God and on behalf of others and creation
- Discuss current economic, political, and social issues, and wonder how the mercy and grace of God affects your response
- Wonder aloud with others how the gods of possessions, consumption, and self-interest get in the way of the God of the cross of Christ Jesus
- Routinely eat meals together with family or friends; this provides valuable time and "kitchen table setting" for the deeper conversations that express care for others and for the passionate convictions of one's life

- Find quiet, relaxing places (i.e., a quiet room in the home, a park, beach, or other setting in nature) to engage in caring conversations that allow for focused attention on the person/people with whom you are speaking
- Have congregational decision meetings (i.e., councils, boards, committees, etc.) in settings conducive to caring conversations about being stewards of the mysteries of God (e.g., people's homes and more informal and cozy congregational settings)
- Go for walks with your conversation partner(s)
- Use FaithTalk® Four Keys, FaithTalk® apps, or some other resource that helps you have conversations that explore the deeper issues and questions of life
- Make sure to share personal and family stories that lift up core values, beliefs, and convictions
- Take advantage of time for service with others as occasions for meaningful conversations, including doing chores around the home, work projects, and ministry trips
- Identify email, Facebook, and text messages that can be followed up by phone and face-to-face conversations

Devotions

- Instead of feeding the insatiable quest for more news and social networking, consider beginning and/or ending the day reading, praying, or meditating on Scripture
- Pray regularly
- Offer action-oriented "prayers of thanksgiving" with your time, talent, and treasure
- Pray the Lord's Prayer regularly
- Use table graces at mealtimes
- Prayerfully seek to experience and see life with the imagination of the gospel, of a world loved to life by God, in Christ, through the Holy Spirit for all time and eternity
- Wonder what God has given you to bless others and creation
- Smile for a divine reason

- Be grateful
- Bless others and creation with word and deed
- Make prayer a central part of your service with and for others and for creation
- Talk about a "God moment" you've had recently. Where and when have you been particularly aware of God's presence and God's activity?
- Fast and use the extra time not digesting food in prayer, Scripture, and discerning how to remember and serve the millions of people who need food

Service

- Open the door for another person, especially an elder or a child
- Make less trash for others to pick up
- Make it easier for others to get from the on-ramp onto the freeway
- Support causes that promote dignity and joy in people and creation
- Help someone up who has fallen
- Develop home and congregational budgets that include narrative accounts of how the dollars serve and celebrate life in Christ. Such narrative budgets foster a climate of generosity.
- Vote
- Learn about issues and injustices that get in the way of others being treated fairly and with mercy
- Imagine someone you judge critically and try to consider life from their perspective
- Learn a trade, a skill, or an academic field so that you can serve others and wink at God as you do it
- Pray for courage. You never know when you will need to use it
- Love God and love neighbor as often as you can remember, and pray that you will remember
- Turn off mean-spirited news casting
- Turn on the joy of serving

- Visit a different culture in your own town or around the world to learn from others
- Look at your income and assets and give until it feels good

Rituals and Traditions

- Sing songs of praise and thanksgiving
- Dance with the Lord of the Dance
- Welcome people in
- Bless people when they come in and when they go out
- Give regularly to organizations that serve the needs of others or creation
- Have religious symbols in your home that express your faith
- Have poems or visual arts on display that remind you of the needs of others
- Keep a piggybank that gathers money for a favorite cause like feeding the hungry, housing the homeless, or caring for creation
- Give safe and caring hugs
- Be open to receive safe and caring hugs
- Smile
- Laugh
- Pray
- Sing in the shower and other places, too

GO DOWNSTAIRS:
THE GIFT OF PRESCHOOLS, DAY SCHOOLS, AND AFTER SCHOOL PROGRAMS

As part of a Vibrant Faith Congregational Training, I interviewed the senior pastor. Though he was filled with excitement and ideas to expand the ministry of the congregation, he bemoaned that the congregation had not learned how to connect with the immediate community. People came from far and wide to be a part of the congregation, but very few came from the more diverse community that lived within walking distance. I responded, "Go downstairs. You have connected with the immediate community and quite effectively. It is your congregation's preschool program."

Preschools are one of the greatest hidden treasures in the life of the church, yet pastors and other congregational leaders underestimate the gift that they have right under their noses. At best, leaders see the program as a wonderful contribution to the community, offering educational, safe, and (hopefully) affordable space for children and comfort and assurance for parents. At worst, congregational leaders and the general membership resent the presence of a preschool or daycare in their building. The overarching perception remains that these programs sap important resources, time, and money, and make the church space way too noisy during the week.

Such school programs need not be at odds with the other work of the congregation. If the home is church, where Christ is present in faith, why not affirm that a congregation's preschool or Christian day school program is church, too? Once congregational leaders and these educational ministry centers recognize that faith development is the common denominator between them, they can more fully appreciate and support one another.

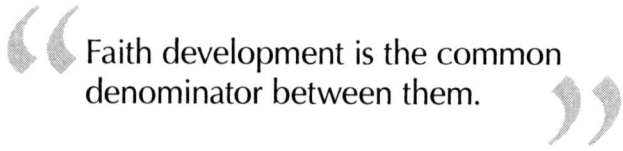

Faith development is the common denominator between them.

Moreover, it is possible to serve a community with diverse religious affiliations and still live out of an evangelical center. For a congregational preschool program that takes the faith seriously nurtures the faith of children and has the capacity to impact the child's home life as well. In fact, a congregational preschool can promote all that can be attained through the Vibrant Faith Frame:

The Six Locations enter into the classroom by caring for the child, the child's home environment, the congregation that supports and equips the child, the immediate surroundings of the child in a supportive community life, by introducing the child to the larger cultural context for life and faith, and by attending to animals, trees, and other parts of God's creation.

The Five Principles are evident in the loving relationships between teachers, other staff, volunteer support staff from the congregation, parents, and children. All these relationships serve as vehicles of the Holy Spirit to pass on the Christian faith. A congregation that has a preschool, day care, or day school can speak of the meaningful partnership between home, congregation, and school. The preschool that lives out the Vibrant Faith Frame addresses not only the child in the classroom but also the child in the home. Equipping the home with educational and faith-formative resources and practices blesses the child and the larger family unit in many ways, including parents who experience an extra measure of delight from a family bonded in Christ. Fostering care between children and with adults at the preschool, offering routine chapel time, and providing tools for the home to nurture the Christian faith and love clearly represents faith that is caught more than it is taught as a classroom lesson alone. Surrounding the children with teachers, support staff, involved parents (involved in the home as well as in the school), and members of the congregation who offer their support during the day gives ample evidence of the fifth principle: "If we want Christian children and youth, we need Christian adults," adults who surround the children with the language and experience of God's love for them.

The Four Keys are the tools that equip the preschool program, the staff and volunteers, as well as the families in the home. Offering the children and the families conversation starters, devotional practices, service ideas, and Christian rituals and traditions demonstrates what a healthy and vibrant faith family looks like. In early childhood, children and their parents are particularly receptive to such suggestions. Children are learning to talk and to use a larger vocabulary more fluently and parent-child conversations are such a natural part of that. Reading to children is a wonderful opportunity to introduce simple stories from storybook Bibles not only for warm conversations but also for devotional time. As children learn how to do more things with their hands and imagination, they are learning the rudimentary tools needed to serve others. And every parent knows how children flourish on rituals, traditions, and routines. Once the children have learned a routine, every parent learns the danger of changing it! This developmental moment certainly provides a valuable occasion to introduce folding one's hands for a table grace, blessing one another with bedtime prayers, weekly gatherings in the congregation, and holiday times like Christmas, Holy Week, and Easter that celebrate the story of the Christian faith.

Preschool director, Brigette Weier, introduced the Four Keys to her staff so that they could use the practices with the children and also get them into the homes of the children. As an example, she had the teachers start a "good-bye blessing" with the children at the parent pick-up time. Weier also introduced a "snack blessing" song at the fall family night event. One mother wrote back to tell of the impact of the faith practices on her daughter, Lizzie, and the entire family:

> *Thank you for all the communications! It is so interesting to be on the other side of all of this . . . I see how crucial it is to get info from the teachers, though Lizzie tells us so much of what happens at school. There are so many awesome things spilling into our home/family that you have introduced. She is very excited that she taught us the blessing song and we sing [it] at all family meals . . . my husband was raised Episcopal and I was raised Catholic, and we both had our own blessings we would say with our families—this is a great new ritual for our family. Love it! Lizzie also shares songs, stories, counting . . . pretty much everything is exciting and motivating to her. THANK YOU!*

It is abundantly evident that this entire family has found in the preschool program far more than simply safe space and age-appropriate learning.

Imagine all the other families eager for something new in their homes that will help them cherish their family life. Most of those families do not have faith traditions to draw upon like the Catholic mother described above. Most families are not even sure what to ask for or how to pursue it. Some families bring their children to Christian preschools hoping their child will get something the parents don't know how to give. Often, the Christian preschool is not aware of these larger possibilities. Preschools committed to the Vibrant Faith Frame can offer much that affects the faith and health of the family life in the home, and will often receive grateful thanks from parents.

Missed Opportunities

Unfortunately, most pastors have not been trained to be aware of these rich possibilities for children, families, and congregations. Nor are they even aware how much the preschools and daycare centers need the pastor's recognition and support. Simply greeting the children and visiting their classrooms on occasion is a great and easy first step.

Some Congregations Do Get It

Salem Lutheran Church in Glendale, California had a day school through the sixth grade. The pastors and leaders welcomed the children into the activities of the congregation, and connected directly and regularly with the school staff and children. Then the leadership went further and reflected on the second of the Five Principles and explored a logo and tag line that identified the local church as a partnership between congregation, home, and school. After all, if the congregation and the home are church, then why not the school, too? And why not promote the presence of the church in the congregation's preschool or after school programs?

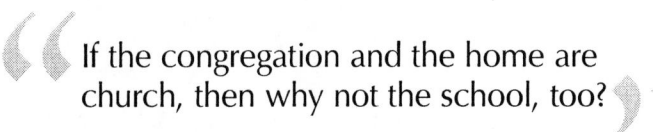

If the congregation and the home are church, then why not the school, too?

When they subsequently developed a capital campaign for their school, leader Joanne Wiedman learned from the alumni of the Salem Lutheran School, six of whom were interviewed on camera for a promotional video. She reports:

> *Since we were considering taking our appeal outside the church community to those in our city who valued a good school irrespective of its religious affiliation, we were seeking comments about the quality of the academic education received.*

> *What we heard surprised us sufficiently that we ended up re-slanting our materials, excited at this information that we considered part of God's direction and our self-discovery in the development process. I can summarize . . . our overall experience.*
>
> *The first repeated theme across interviewees: a Christian school as the third leg of faith development (in addition to religious guidance at home and in the congregation) was key, they believed, to the development of their Christian faith. Salem did this effectively, they held, because the faith was not presented as religious dogma; rather [the children] were taught at every turn of a loving God who valued them uniquely, and they were cared for by teachers and staff who reinforced this daily. God's love was shown concretely, in the name of the church, during a developmental stage at which it is highly important that the message [children] are taught and the evidence they see lived out is consistent.*

The second repeated theme: Each to a person hoped their own children could receive the same kind of integrated education they had received at Salem, so key did they consider their primary education at Salem to their adult faith development.

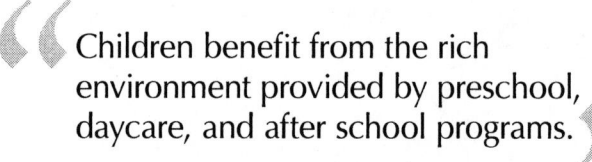

Children benefit from the rich environment provided by preschool, daycare, and after school programs.

The conclusions are clear: children benefit from the rich environment provided by preschool, daycare, and after school programs. Not only that, the families of the children benefit, too. The congregation is energized knowing that its God-given gifts bless the larger community, whether or not the children and families are members of the congregation. And families that experience the blessings of the congregation through the preschool, daycare, or after school just might find reason to connect more fully with the life of the congregation in other ways, too.

The idea of the congregation connecting with the preschool (or other school-related program) in a meaningful way is not new; it has just not been actively promoted or developed in the church. Retired Pastor Roger Skatrud is one of those people who got the point decades ago. His congregation had a preschool and he and his pastoral colleague connected with the children and the staff on a regular basis. Every class period of the preschool ended with a set ritual and tradition, which included caring conversation and devotions. The congregation also established the tradition of making the office of the two pastors available to the kids after preschool ended. The children loved to run to the pastors' offices—and they did run! They lined up by a pastor's desk to get their reward, a stamp on the back of their hands that read, "God's." They also engaged in conversations with the pastors, who routinely told each child he or she was God's child, and that they were very happy that that particular child was at the preschool to learn about how God loved them and to make other friends that God loved. The office secretary soon got into the routine as well by providing a little treat for the children when they came to the church office, but the first thing the kids wanted was their stamp.

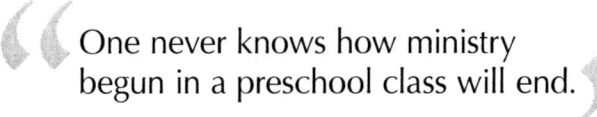

One never knows how ministry begun in a preschool class will end.

Pastor Skatrud recalled one child in particular who liked the stamp. She had major health problems and was in and out of the hospital. The stamp reminded her and her family that she was not damaged goods or somehow less than any other child. Eventually the little girl lost her fight for life. As family and friends gathered around her coffin, one last time Pastor Skatrud stamped on her hand, "God's," epitomizing the message everyone needed to receive that day. One never knows how ministry begun in a preschool class will end. Having the Christian faith as an active part of any preschool can offer benefits that last a lifetime, no matter how long that lifetime may be.

Grace Lutheran Church in Hendersonville, NC likewise has been experimenting with and developing its preschool program. The pastors and other staff welcome the preschool families with open arms. They inform the families that even if they have another church family, Grace Lutheran considers them part of their church family. The parents have entrusted the congregation with their most precious gifts, their children and Grace Lutheran considers it a privilege and a deep responsibility to care for those children by providing safe space, a rich educational and social environment, and a place where the Christian faith is central to all they do. The congregation understands that caregiving to include not only cognitive, social, and physical development, but also spiritual development[1].

> To care for the whole life development of the child includes attending to the child's home life.

The staff makes it clear that to care for the whole life development of the child includes attending to the child's home life. So throughout the year, Grace Lutheran Preschool equips the home with suggestions and resources that serve and bless the life of the child in the home with parent(s) and other siblings. As an example of this larger care for the child and the more holistic approach of the preschool program, the congregation offers a parenting class that is directed primarily to the families in the preschool program but also includes parents from the congregation. It is another way Grace Lutheran shows that the life and faith of the homes of the preschool children are highly valued and cared for.

The parenting class is entitled Passing On the Faith (POF) and concentrates on the faith life of the home. The pastors teach that the family's faith life impacts not only the children but the entire family, and that what the pastors and preschool program are nurturing is not only the Christian faith but the family life dynamics and relationships themselves. The pastors teach what they have done in their own homes and with their own children. They have the families practice examples of things that can be done throughout the year, paying special attention to how to celebrate the seasons of the church year like Advent and Christmas. Most everything they teach utilizes the Four Keys. The congregation has a Vibrant Faith Ministries Resource Center with numerous resources that parents can purchase for use in the home. Some of those resources are used in the POF classes so that parents can feel more comfortable using these faith-forming and family-building tools in their own homes.

One of the favorite items to teach is how to bless children on a regular basis. Pastor Langsford observed that one mom began to give a blessing to her child when the child was taken to the preschool classroom. Before long, all the other kids were standing in line each day to be blessed by this same mother.

> Their preschool program exits as a significant form of church to those families.

When the congregation was in its second year of teaching the POF classes to the preschool program parents as well as the parents who are members of the congregation, it discovered that 31 of the 70 families did not list a church affiliation. Whether or not any of those 31 families eventually joins the weekly worship life of the congregation or even become members is not the primary concern of Grace Lutheran.

Rather, the leadership of the congregation is aware that their preschool program exits as a significant form of church to those families, families that want and need valuable care for their children and their larger family life. The staff and other leaders want all 70 families to be excited to come home each day, knowing that their home is holy ground. Grace Lutheran equips the families with resources and experiences that show how precious their home is in the sight of God as a place for the preschool children and all their families to grow—including to grow in the love and grace of God.

As a congregation that has gone through the Vibrant Faith Congregational Training and coaching for the pastors, Grace Lutheran is committed to doing research to learn how the strategies and programs are working. As a part of that process, the pastors have solicited feedback from parents in the POF class. The information from one family was particularly noteworthy. The wife and mother stated that, although she was raised in the church and even attended a Christian school through the eighth grade, in the past she had left her faith life at the congregation. She and her husband are now instituting faith life practices in the home that she wishes she had had as a child. The couple has twins who are two, plus a three-year old. The parents acknowledge that at bedtime it "can be insanity," but they also note that the addition of bedtime prayers has had a calming affect on both of them. They write of the new bedtime routine, "We were all better for it, parents and kids." The children have begun to expect prayers at bedtime. If the parents are running late or are exhausted and forget, the kids holler, "It's time to pray," or "We didn't pray." Devotions are now part of their family time. In spite of all the children's books on the shelf, it is "the Jesus book" (the toddler Bible given by the congregation at the time of baptism) that the children ask for. The impact on the family has been so significant that the husband insisted that the couple send in their comments to the pastor. He wanted them to know how much the congregation's efforts have impacted his family.

The couple acknowledges that even when they do not make it to worship on Sundays at Grace, they do not feel as though they have left God out of their lives for the week. "It has made a huge difference for us. If we miss a worship service on Sunday morning, it is nice to know we have not missed God for the week," for God is part of their family all week long. They write:

> *Suggestions from this class have led us to change our children's bedtime routines, adding nighttime prayers and saying, "God bless" for anyone who had touched our lives or is in need of prayer. This has helped us transition the kids from the hectic day to a calming bedtime. . . the sound of three toddlers reciting "Now I lay me down to sleep . . . " is absolutely priceless. It's in those moments that you feel God's presence. . . . This program has encouraged us to be more involved in the church. We meet "friendly faces" in a small group who we also see on Sundays. That makes going to church feel more like a community. This program served as a "jumpstart" for us to start attending church regularly. . . . [and it] opened up communication between us . . . We've had discussion about rituals we did as children that were very important that we would like to continue with our children. . . . This program has helped us prioritize our children's activities and take time for what is important. Even during very busy times we are more likely to make time for our faith.*

Grace Lutheran has also used the Vibrant Faith Frame with their after school program. The children come and are greeted by their own study buddy, an adult who engages them in conversation, helps them with homework, and takes time for Bible reading and prayer. It, too, has become a great success for the ministry of the congregation. This cross+generational midweek program has produced results never before imagined. What follows are some of the comments by the participants themselves. Notice how the Five Principles, Four Keys, and AAA Christian Disciples are evident in the words and experiences these people share.

My study buddy was Ms. Betsy. I really enjoyed it. Ms. Betsy found out I liked science and for many weeks she would bring things to do experiments. It was fun and I learned new things. When I wanted a husky, we read husky books and listed good and bad things. I found out they were too big and that Mom may be allergic to them. I knew the Bible Stories we read, so we decided to draw pictures of them and write a summary story on the back. We have lots of fun. I hope Ms. Betsy is my study buddy next year!
Sandi

Recently I retired from teaching and when study buddies began this year it certainly sounded like something that I would enjoy doing. It has proven to be just that. I have worked with children for years and understand that relationship that can develop because of one-on-one time together. Each week we have time to learn about each other and, consequently, I have made a new best friend. Sandi is very athletic and loves to play soccer and I look forward to attending some of her games. I enjoy supporting her areas of interest...science, writing, and animals. She has grown academically – and I feel both of us have grown spiritually as a result of our time together. Whenever I see Sandi, her welcoming, beautiful smile and her cheerfulness make my day. I will definitely be a study buddy next year and would encourage others to consider it. It is one of the most fulfilling experiences I have had and the rewards are monumental!
Betsy

My Study Buddy has been an inspiration to me. Just seeing his enthusiasm to learn and his active imagination makes even a "mature" adult become more "alive." It is a pleasure to have a small part in his formal education. Brings back fond memories.
Harold

My experience with my study buddy, Jenny, has been such a pleasure. It has been a privilege to spend time with Olivia doing homework, working on research, and just chatting. The program connects adults with students and widens the experiences of both participants. This allows all of us to show our Christian spirit through our behavior. These connections last a lifetime for each and every one of us. I feel blessed to have been involved in this project.
Patty

Study Buddies has been a wonderful experience for my daughter. Not only does she get to catch up on the week's homework, but she also has made a new friend in her adult study buddy who has given her lots of encouragement and support in her journey to her First Communion.
Heather Anderson and Hannah

It's been a very exciting and rewarding last few months. You get a chance to share your faith with an excitable, willing-to-learn young person and to outwardly live your faith so they will hopefully see and feel Christ's love through you. You watch them grow, learn, and hopefully develop a trusting, mutual respect for each other. The outward expression of missing you or seeing you is very rewarding.
Don

My time as a study buddy with 6–year-old (now 7!!) Kirsti has been a blessing for me. Every Wednesday's time with her reminds me of Jesus telling the crowd, "Let the children come unto me". She is so eager in her learning to read and things of nature she has learned at school. She generally selects the Bible story to read. Our half hour flies by! And then we share a special quiet prayer and hold hands as we tell [God] THANK YOU for this blessing of time together.

The mother of a third grader was so moved by the care and attention given her daughter that the mother volunteered to be a kidney donor for the study buddy's diabetic husband. Although the mother did not end up being a match as a kidney donor, her willingness to make the sacrifice was a moving gesture to the study buddy and her husband. Because of her gesture and that of others from the congregation, the husband began to participate in the life of the congregation in ways he never had before, including taking Holy Communion for the first time in eighteen years. The wife has noticed that her husband's faith life has been strengthened in other ways, too, and the couple has grown closer to one another.

The same adult study buddy was impressed and delighted by the third grader in her charge. When the adult would make a mistake helping the student, the third grader would say, "That's alright, everyone makes mistakes." At one time the older study buddy made a card for her young friend. The girl responded with her own card and wrote, "Thank you for your thoughtfulness. A kind deed is like water for a flower: it makes the heart bloom. Thanks for planting a garden in my heart." The adult was convinced that her younger friend had wisdom beyond her years. Having the younger friend was also of help to the elder. Because of her husband's illness, having a study buddy was also a great outlet for her.

Congregations can also invest in the community through day school and alternative school programs. In one case, a congregation initiated a relationship with the school district to donate space for work with homebound students who were part of an alternative school for high school students struggling academically and socially.

Sometimes such investment in the community has unexpected consequences. At one point in the second year of the program, a student brought in a gun to the church building and alternative school classroom. The congregation was understandably alarmed and conversations ensued regarding the future of the program within the church walls. The congregation's quilters, older women who gather weekly to make quilts for global distribution, met down the hall from the classroom and became very anxious when they heard about the gun. However, after discussing the issues for some time, the congregation continued to welcome in the students and the quilters ended up teaching the students how to make quilts. Instead of staring at the students anxiously, the group of quilters welcomed their newfound friends with glad smiles.

The program worked so well that it outgrew the congregation's facilities. At the end of the year, the Alternative Program Coordinator sent a thank you letter and stated, "We were truly blessed to have the church space to build our program . . . It's been an incredible year! One with many new adventures, many positive steps forward into the future and some rough patches along the way. Through it all, we hung together as a 'family' to persevere and became much stronger individuals and a program because of it all." The coordinator listed statistics of success in the program, including a 93% increase in class attendance. One can only wonder how much of that was due to the congregation's hospitable environment, including the quilters. The Program Coordinator ended her comments with an exhortation to continue to reach out to the young people of today, people of need who are also people of talent and promise.

Another congregation started an after-school mentoring program with a nearby middle school, and each year hosted a Christmas party for the mentors and students. The mentoring program eventually grew to encompass the entire school district and expanded beyond the capacities of the efforts of the single congregation. Most all the congregations in the school district joined in this educational and community effort.[2] It is another example of people in a congregation seeing a need, responding, and creating a supportive environment for children and youth to mature in a cross+generational setting.

> Creating a supportive environment for children and youth to mature in a cross+generational setting.

This chapter has suggested a few of the many ways for a congregation to be a missional presence in the larger community, a presence that teaches, preaches, and embodies grace and mercy in Christ in word and deed. It can be through the care of small children and their families in a preschool program. It can be through caring for school children and youth in day school and after school programs. Whatever the way to connect with young people in the formative years of life, these opportunities establish a strong link between faith and daily life, between the church that impacts people in a positive way and the needs of children, youth and their families. Such opportunities are well worth pursuing. Where they already exist, their power to nurture faith and healthy relationships is to be honored and honed by staff, lay leadership, and the larger congregational community.

CONGREGATIONAL ADMINISTRATION

For many people, the administrative aspect of congregational ministry can seem less than inspiring. Realize that the root meaning of *administrate* is simply 'to serve' and what seemed tedious and mundane becomes another way in which to proclaim the gospel to the world.

A cornerstone text for administration could be Ephesians 4:11-12: "The gifts he gave were that some would be apostles, some prophets, some evangelists, some pastors and teachers, to equip the saints for the work of ministry, for building up the body of Christ." The list is obviously not an exhaustive list of spiritual gifts; indeed, there is a different list of gifts in Romans 12:6-8 and 1 Corinthians 12:8-10, 28-30. It does, however, identify a key ingredient for the gifts of the Spirit: to serve larger efforts "for building up the body of Christ," or, as Paul puts it in 1 Corinthians 12:7, "for the common good." These gifts are meant not to shine a light on the gifted individual but on the larger needs of the community both within and beyond the church.

First Corinthians 12:28 includes in the list of spiritual gifts a category of "forms of assistance, forms of leadership" that the RSV translates as "helpers and administrators," the kinds of positions not necessarily gifted to preach the gospel but still important to lead a community so that the preaching and teaching of the gospel can happen effectively. Without the gifts for administration, how can any Christian ministry happen effectively?

Administration is the support ministry for the work of the larger calling of the body of Christ to go and make disciples. Even when such ministry takes the form of behind–the–scenes paper work, it is filled with the Spirit of God and essential to building up the body of Christ. Therefore, administration has vast implications for the care and support of servant-leaders and leadership teams, the use of media to communicate the ministry of the congregation, and the motivation of others to be equipped for ministry. Like all ministries, the heart of administration is to remind individuals, homes, and the larger congregational system that the church exists for those not yet part of the church. Ineffective administration that sees its primary task as "keeping the doors open" misses the point of having the doors open to a world of need and a world of joyous response.

What Can Be Gained by the Vibrant Faith Frame?

This chapter focuses on how to establish and maintain a faith-focused administration through the constant application of the Vibrant Faith Frame and particularly the Four Key faith practices. The Five Principles will also loom large, as congregational servant-leaders are mindful of the relational nature of the Christian faith and the life of the church that reaches deeply into homes to reach back out to the larger world. Healthy congregations lead with servant-leaders who are themselves faithful AAA disciples, not simply functionaries who know how to get things done and keep things running.

The goal of good administrators is not simply doing head counts and making and keeping to budgets but lives transformed by the gospel. This change in culture will not happen simply because people want it to happen. It occurs as wise leaders articulate over and over again a clear and doable vision of church that partners home and congregation to reach individuals, households, congregation, community, culture, and into the vast reaches of creation itself. It happens because a sense of gospel urgency and necessity surrounds the decisions and actions of the congregation.

This change in culture happens because people see how the Christian faith makes a difference in people's lives. We hear stories of how various groups within the congregation—groups such as staff, leadership teams, ministry groups, prayer and Bible study groups, and households—begin to own the Vibrant Faith Frame and work to edify people's lives in Christ. It happens as the Vibrant Faith Frame begins to shape the lives of servant leaders and rouses the larger community of faith to define itself as a missional church. Such a church understands that it exists to serve and heal life in response to the gospel of Jesus Christ.

Simple Examples

How might a church serve and shape a community in this way? Here are a few simple examples:

Newsletters, Websites, Bulletin Announcements, and Other Forms to Communicate the Congregation's Ministry

A congregation's newsletter, website, and bulletin announces what the congregation is up to, its planned activities, and the needs of individuals, families, and larger communities. Besides the occasional thank-you note, rarely do newsletters report on how the lives of people have been changed. People need to hear and read how the ministry of a congregation actually makes a difference. To know that the Four Keys have brought joy to individuals and households elevates one's attention to the value of the Vibrant Faith Frame. These stories of transformational change articulate the vision and faith practices of the congregation over and over again and motivate others to value and apply that vision and practices to their own lives.

It is one thing to announce that the congregation will now have the Taking Faith Home (TFH) sheet available each week in the bulletin or narthex. It is another to learn how using the TFH Four Key ideas brought tears to a father's eyes or helped grandparents connect as faith mentors with their grandchildren. It has consequences for people to learn that board members look forward to each monthly meeting because using the TFH as a group helps them nurture their Christian faith as they talk, pray, and serve with others committed to the gospel. These stories create a climate of change that others want to join. It exemplifies faith formed by the power of the Holy Spirit through personal, trusted relationships. But if no one in the congregation knows that the Four Keys have influenced anything, why would people give the Holy Spirit a second chance through TFH?[1]

Location Matters: Meeting in Homes

Because of the Vibrant Faith Frame, a pastor changed the congregation's typical fall stewardship drive. He invited groups of 40 to meet together to experience the Four Keys. The goal was to excite people in a community of faith through experiences of Christian care and hospitality. To emphasize that the church is not simply in church buildings, the groups met in people's homes to discuss individual hopes and dreams as well as the larger ministry of the congregation. The Four Keys structured the home meetings. One of the surprises for the pastor is that people came who were not even invited, people who had been members of the congregation but had not participated in the life of the congregation for some time. This pastor discovered that in those more informal and intimate settings of homes of friends, others felt free to participate. The meetings served as a concrete example of how the home is church to people in ways that the congregation could only dream. An administrative decision to use the Vibrant Faith Frame to redesign a fall stewardship campaign—one where financial stewardship was not even on the agenda—helped a congregation reach out to people, ideas, and passions not otherwise accessible.

Administration and Congregational Hospitality

Administrative leadership impacts the fabric of the congregation's hospitality as well. Christian hospitality is always close to the surface of the life of a congregation and lives out the Four Keys in concrete ways. That spirit of welcome influences the thinking and actions of staff and lay volunteers as well as the larger goals of church administration.

A Sexton

A Vibrant Faith congregational trainer interviewed a congregational staff in Billings, Montana. The staff enjoyed talking about their custodian who loved his work and communicated to others the love of God through it. It was evident in his work at the congregation, day in and day out. He himself acknowledged that when he opened the doors in the morning, he prayed for all who would enter the building that day, people like those in the AA groups, youth and adults in the scouting program, people needing emergency help, as well as staff and congregational members going about their various ministry tasks.

As the conversations continued, the trainer suggested that the congregation change the title of the position from custodian to sexton, a term some church bodies give to those who care for church facilities as a matter of faith and public ministry. Historically, the sexton was a minor clergy in charge of the care of property. A form of congregational administration is the care of building space so that people can use various rooms with the goal of serving others with the gospel in word and deed. The care for and cleaning of space can be a job hired out to a janitorial services firm, and that can work, too, but someone from the congregation might feel called to take on the same tasks as a ministry. Congregational administration through the services of a sexton represents another example of building up the body of Christ, of service for the common good. It also reflects that the Christian faith that can be taught by a loving sexton as well as by a Sunday school teacher.

A Receptionist

Terrie is the receptionist at a large congregation in the suburbs of the Twin Cities in Minnesota. The caller can imagine her smile just from the tone of voice on the phone. Gatekeepers like Terrie have the important task of embodying the entire congregation's welcome so it is well to find someone who is as genuine in her welcome as Terrie. Congregational administration is service to equip the saints for the work of the church, and the work of the church involves outreach and hospitality. By word and deed, effective administrators communicate to the larger world the message, "People are welcome here." Administration is a gift of the Spirit that builds up the body of Christ, including its outreach to others. Attention to the outreach element of administration requires attention to warm hospitality toward stranger and friend alike.

Ushers, Greeters, and Event Hosts

The administrative tasks of anticipating and managing well-planned hospitality also influence areas like worship and Christian education classes. Ushers and greeters have a larger role than handing out bulletins along with a warm handshake. When people arrive who are new to the congregation, a well-trained usher can make sure that the newcomer is connected to a worshipper who can help put them at ease during and after the worship service. Some people will walk into a worship setting for the first time and want minimal assistance while others will want more care and attention. The worshipping community can learn to adjust to the wants and needs of visitors. A greeter can make an important contribution to a visitor by finding the visitor after worship to make that person welcome and determine if there is interest in joining others for casual conversation following the service. Sometimes congregants gather in a designated fellowship space that is not always so accessible, visible, or inviting. Guiding a person and walking alongside that person down the hall or down the stairs can be a true act of grace. Congregations intentional about hospitality for those joining them in worship will want to pay administrative attention to how to make that happen as seamlessly as possible.

A senior pastor tried in vain to get the associate pastor to create a hospitable climate for a new member class. The associate pastor was a very good teacher and well versed in the content he was presenting to the new members. But the senior pastor wanted the new members to experience that the congregation valued community warmth and informality as well as substance and meaningful information for daily life and faith. He hoped that softer lighting, relaxing music in the background, and tablecloths covered with fresh fruit and other appetizers would send a message of invitation, tranquility, and welcome. However, the gift of being a host continued to elude the pastor in charge of new member classes.

What the associate pastor needed was someone to assist by orchestrating a hospitable environment. That helper could establish a more welcoming space by welcoming people, and softening the institutional feel of the space with lighting, fabrics, and food.

New Pastor Syndrome

Being a pastor includes an administrative function that many pastors learn through "on the job training." Marie was a new pastor, enthusiastic, committed, and serious about congregational ministry and the role of the gospel in people's lives. Marie was excited about giving Bibles to children as a Milestones Ministry offering of the congregation. (See pp. 37-44 for an explanation of Milestones Ministry.) An important part of the preparation for the Milestone Ministry event was helping parents and other supportive adults to read the Bible regularly with the children about to receive the Bibles. The only problem was that hardly any of the adults showed up for the training prior to the Sunday distribution of Bibles. The pathetically low turnout left Pastor Marie feeling frustrated and like "the wind was taken out of my sails." It didn't help that the office secretary had said earlier, "Good luck," with a tone of disbelief at the thought of getting parents to show up for a multiple-session training on how to open up and use the Bible in one's own home.

Pastor Marie described her many efforts to get the word out: she had sent out postcards, put the invitation on the website and in the newsletter, and made announcements regarding the training during worship, but all to no avail. She did admit, without prompting, that she had not made any phone calls.

Marie was open to exploring alternative ways to communicate and motivate people to come. She learned that written invitations on websites and in newsletters don't motivate. Even a personal postcard lacks the personal contact offered by a face-to-face invitation or personal phone call. Financial development leaders know that if you want someone to make a commitment such as a pledge of finances or time, addressing that person as part of larger groups doesn't feel very personal or real. To invite everyone at once feels like not being invited at all. It is time for us church leaders to use the power of a personal contact and invitations.

To reflect on the disappointing experience, this new pastor proceeded to pose a whole host of unanswered questions like, "What kept them away?" "What would motivate parents to show up?" "When is the best time to offer parental training sessions?" "How many sessions are parents willing to attend?" "What information and skills do parents want for their spiritual leadership in the home?" But she had to do more than guess at the answers. Pastor Marie's recent seminary training had equipped her to do serious research by asking good questions, analyzing human dynamics through case studies, engaging active listening skills, doing team building, developing cross+generational and cross-cultural community building, and creating opportunities for teachable moments. She now had to call on that education to do the work of church administration, in this case discovering how to connect with parents in an effective way to build up the body of Christ. She is planning to do ethnographic study of the congregation through face-to-face, one-on-one, and small group interviews. She wants to learn so she can serve. This is the ministry of effective administration.

Clarify Assumptions and Expectations

People enter into congregational life and specific congregational assignments with a whole host of assumptions and expectations for themselves and others. Those assumptions and expectations can easily clash. Congregational leadership that keeps the process of decision making transparent through candid and caring conversations can balance the diverse wants and needs that no one person or group can satisfy. Transparency fosters humility and cooperation.

One brand new pastor was told during his first month in the congregation that he needed to rewrite the entire confirmation program. He received this assignment from the Christian education chairperson in August. The new confirmation year began the next month. The pastor had been told that the old program had not worked; parents and students didn't like it, so he was urged to try something different. The timing was awful, but this new pastor did the best job he could and within a month was ready to try something new.

The problem was that no one else knew he had been given that assignment. What seemed to him to be a nearly impossible task to pull off in a month, especially for a new pastor, many members of the congregation perceived as an act of pastoral arrogance. They thought he was throwing out the established confirmation program to do something of his own liking. Experiences like this impaired his pastoral leadership. For more than a year, no one knew that the pastor had been told to create a new confirmation program, an assignment that had thrown him into a panic. And he didn't know that key leaders were angry at him for dumping their confirmation program. The expectations and assumptions regarding the confirmation program were wildly divergent, and it cost the new pastor a major hit on his reputation as a caring shepherd.

Wise administration keeps such communications as transparent as possible. When communications are transparent, a congregation's shared vision can be referred to often and connected openly to individual assignments and congregational strategies. The congregation is not just the pastor's—or other leader's—private plaything. So review assignments; get feedback on people's expectations and assumptions regarding assignments; ask questions to get various perspectives; slow down the process to bring in various thoughts and opinions. Leading with transparency and data-seeking questions can calm a system down and take a lot of pressure off individual leaders and leadership teams.

Start with the Leaders

Communicating and living a congregation's shared vision serves as an essential guide for the work of effective administration. Congregational servant-leaders can rush ahead to clearly defined objectives and miss the larger ministry expressed in the shared vision. A custodian can grumble and frown at the children and adults that "make a mess" of the floors and walls while forgetting the importance of wanting to provide clean and hospitable space that encourages people to show up in the first place. A paid staff member or ministry volunteer can answer the phone promptly but convey an attitude of being interrupted instead of being available to serve. An usher can hand out a bulletin but leave a newcomer standing alone and feeling otherwise lost. A conscientious instructor can teach a lesson but leave the students feeling undervalued and unengaged. And a new pastor can express enthusiasm to work with parents but end up communicating frustration because not enough of them showed up. An administrative priority that continues to lift up the value of the Vibrant Faith Frame through trusted relationships and Christian hospitality can enrich a lot of sound church office management, worship preparations, lesson plans, and equipping the body of Christ for ministry.

The Four Keys Set a Tone

Congregational boards, councils, presbyteries, or vestries come together to make decisions that promote the congregation's ministry of Christian faith and outreach. And yet decisions can happen in a way that leaves the leadership frustrated, isolated, and generally disconnected from the very faith the leaders want to celebrate and value. In the midst of the desire to make the best decisions possible, conflicts can ensue, relationships can become frayed, and leaders can begin to count the days until they are off the team and able to walk away from the church. Being an elected leader of a congregation can be an opportunity to deepen one's life of faith, but it also has the potential to make that person a more likely candidate to join the "inactives" following her or his term of office.

One pastor used the Vibrant Faith Frame to help a church council to be fed by the very faith the leaders were trying to support. He writes:

I knew that our Vibrant Faith Ministry was beginning to transform our "culture" as a congregation when the following experience occurred at a monthly meeting of our congregation council.

As the new Senior Pastor of our 167-year-old congregation, I was encouraged by [the VFM coach] to introduce the Four Keys into our congregation council meetings. I decided to begin with the way we conduct caring conversations around the Scriptures during the devotional time.

Actually, like most congregation councils, we've not allowed for much conversation during the devotions. Usually, a well-meaning council member comes prepared to read a small passage from a Christian devotional book, prays a written prayer, and that's it.

In a previous meeting the newly elected council agreed to give this "Four Key thing" a try, but only if I was willing to help the assigned member prepare in advance.

Mary Ann and I met briefly after worship to plan a conversation based upon the Second Lesson of the assigned texts for that Sunday: Hebrews 11:1-3, 8-16. It speaks of the journeys of Abraham and Sarah with God. After reading this text she was going to lead us through two questions:

1. (5 minutes) Ask council members to move into groups of three. Ask each person in the triad to share a particular moment when God was very present to them during a time in their life journey. (Examples might include a job choice, divorce, death of spouse, illness, etc.)

2. (5 minutes) Reconvene the council. Ask council members to speak of a time when God seemed especially present in the life of our congregation.[2]

When the council convened on Tuesday evening, Mary Ann announced that we were going to reflect with one another on the second lesson from last Sunday, and I could see a few people roll their eyes. And yet, as directed, they moved into triads and after a few moments of hesitation, they did the assigned task…slowly. After a while they began to speak more passionately of God's presence in their lives during their journeys of faith—and they did so out loud, to one another, with deep conviction…

Mary Ann interrupted their conversations to bring us together to ask the second question; "Speak of a time when God seemed especially present in this faith community." Instead of asking for volunteers, she went right around this table of fifteen council members, and nodded for each to speak… And they did… The responses were varied—from the baptism of a daughter, to the involvement with a Habitat for Humanity build, to the very decision to run for election to the congregation council itself.

And then we came full circle, to our council chair, the retired executive of a very successful manufacturing company. I'd known him as a quiet, devoted, hard-working servant in our congregation—someone who had hung in there during some turbulent times in our congregation's history. And yet, in his working days, he was known for his toughness—for issuing orders and making demands upon his staff. I wasn't certain how he felt about holding these caring conversations in our council meetings…

Sitting next to me, he paused for a moment, put his face in his hands, and began to shake with quiet sobs…Choking through the tears, he said, "You all know the turmoil and pain we've been through in this church these last several years. But that all ended when Pastor came to serve us."

Encouraging leaders to speak openly and honestly about their faith can help to set a tone of deep fellowship and loving community. It makes some room for the Spirit to do its work.

There were some watery eyes around that boardroom table that night. I suspect our council meetings will never be quite the same... I'm looking forward to next month's meeting. I'm looking forward to the presence of God, with us, at that table....

This pastor refused to take much credit for what was discussed that night and his role in the newfound positive attitude in the congregation. He did acknowledge that, "pastors can help to set a tone." Leadership processes and goals can set a tone. It is part of good, sound administrative leadership. Commitment to the care and faith formation of leaders through open conversations that reflect upon the Scriptures and basic questions of how God might be at work in people's lives can deeply affect servant-leaders. This pastor promoted an administrative step that made a church council more than an administrative arm of the congregation. It became a place for disciples to explore how God's presence can make a difference to individuals and a leadership team.

A pastor was asked by his Vibrant Faith Ministries coach to begin to have one-on-one Four Key experiences with his staff members. He was also asked to help individual council members to prepare for the monthly council devotions. This particular pastor was a trained spiritual director but had never thought about using that training with his own staff and council in such a personal way. One by one he sat down with his staff members and council leaders to discuss not only their congregational assignments but also their journeys of faith, including how their faith was being affected by their time as a congregational servant-leader. The pastor was amazed at how quickly people responded to the new style of pastoral leadership.

Although there were initial hesitations and suspicions, especially by the staff members, those quickly subsided as the genuineness of the pastor's care enabled new conversations between pastor and staff members and pastor and council leaders. One council member was particularly quiet at council meetings. The pastor had very little idea of what was in that council member's head and heart. He was amazed at what he learned once he sat down with that council member alone. It deepened the pastor's appreciation for the faith and service of this quiet council member. One staff member stated that the conversation with the pastor was well timed because of some soul searching that she knew she needed to do. It was a concern that the pastor had no idea the staff member was wrestling with. The pastor wondered aloud to his coach: "What have I been doing the past twenty years [by not engaging in this kind of pastoral care and leadership]?"

Offering spiritual leadership to a council or board and providing pastoral care to a congregation's staff have not been the way most pastors have been trained to get things done. It is a form of administrative leadership that has been sadly neglected. As a consequence, leaders have experienced their own faith crises without support, and tense leadership relationships have persisted that could have been addressed prior to major eruptions.

Exit Interviews

Exit interviews are another example of pastoral and congregational leadership that has in mind healthy care of souls and that attends to the formation of faith of the leaders who serve in the congregation. When individuals finish terms on leadership teams or staff members resign their positions, it is a good time to offer an exit interview that does more than conduct a performance appraisal. Such transitions provide opportunities to explore the deeper meaning and experiences of people's time of service to the body of Christ, their joys and sorrows, their sense of accomplishments, failures, and disappointment. The realities of community life in a congregation can be just as messy as any other community experience, and perhaps even more so. An exit interview that allows time to celebrate the joys, acknowledge new insights, and admit, confess, and receive forgiveness for mistakes and misdeeds along the way are all part of Christian shepherding process. The Four Keys can structure these exit interviews to provide caring conversations that review people's experiences and devotionally connect those experiences to the good news of Jesus Christ. The interview is an important service and an occasion to name the service of those departing a particular role in the congregation. The very process of offering prayers of thanksgiving, confession, and forgiveness expresses the heart of the gospel life and Christian tradition. The Four Keys set a tone for congregational leadership at all stages of that leadership in the life of the congregation.

Leading for Faith Formation

At some point most congregational leadership will feel like it is getting off track and is stuck in a rut, that it is doing the work of the church more as a matter of course than as a ministry of grace, mercy, and peace. Staff members can begin to feel disconnected from colleagues and others active in the life of the congregation. Elected and appointed leaders in the congregation can find their schedules more filled with meetings and agendas than their lives in touch with the word of God and the presence of God. Here is the place for the foundational faith practices of the Four Keys to shape the life of the ministry of the congregation.

At Morning Star Lutheran Church the pastors have made a concerted effort to groom the leaders and larger congregation with the word of God heard and practiced through the Four Keys. Each month a council member reflects on the Four Keys by using the Taking Faith Home bulletin insert that has examples of each of the Four Keys, daily Bible readings, and weekly prayers and meditations. The assigned council member uses the Taking Faith Home to guide a devotional at the beginning of the meeting.

The pastors also did this kind of devotional piece at a council meeting to introduce the practice and to give an example of how easy it can be. The senior pastor asks for a copy of what the council member has offered and edits it for use in the next month's newsletter. It is a way for the congregation to benefit from the devotional used at the council meeting as well as from the faith life of the council member.

What follows is an example of a council member doing what he first saw modeled by his pastors:

I would like to share with you our family's use of Taking Faith Home for the week of February 14.

Scripture Verse for the Week: Luke 9:35 "A voice came from the cloud. It said, "This is my Son, and I have chosen him. Listen to him."

Now, it is mostly Diane and me...and thank God I am not traveling as much as I did. Our use of Taking Faith Home is occasional at best but this is what we are "Taking On For Lent". So for this week, the start of Lent, we immersed ourselves by using all Four Keys.

- *For **Devotional** Practices, we attended Ash Wednesday Worship.*

- *For **Rituals and Traditions**, we ate a Pancake and Sausage dinner on Shrove Tuesday.*

- *And for **Service** we decided to drink only water during Lent and contribute the money we would spend on coffee, tea, cokes, etc. to Haiti Relief.*

*But for me the most meaningful focus this week was **Caring Conversation**:*

- *Why is it important to listen to others? What is the difference between hearing and listening?*

- *God the Father tells us to listen to his Son, Jesus. What does it mean to listen to Jesus?*

We really had a good discussion about the obvious differences between hearing and listening. Diane and I both identified two key points:

- *Pay attention when someone is speaking and be sure you understand what the other person said and means.*

- *Respond to what is communicated and follow up on what has been communicated.*

For me I need to stop talking and thinking about what I am going to say or do in response and just listen. But ultimately, listening to someone means determining what and how to respond and then responding. Our relationship with each other depends on listening to each other. Diane and I both are confident that God hears us and He listens to us. We hear Him. Now we will focus during Lent to listen to Him.

This example shows how meaningful yet simple it is to offer congregations helpful tools for personal and family devotions. It shows that congregational leaders are not just people of decision-making power but elders of the faith who influence the spiritual life of congregations. Too often congregational leadership teams like councils, boards, vestries, or presbyteries have operated in a way that seems more like a corporation than a church. The primary role of these leadership organizations felt more like making sure staff and lay volunteers are working on and accomplishing assignments than doing the larger work of the spiritual care of the congregation that includes prayerful discernment of the ministry of the congregation and support of those engaged in those ministries. There is a big difference between a board watching to make sure the pastor puts in enough hours and walking alongside the pastor as a spiritual elder caring for the entire congregation's spiritual, mental, physical, fiscal, and emotional health. Council devotions that encourage faith practices that the entire congregation can use shifts the center of attention away from council motions and votes to the spiritual care of the larger faith community.

These examples of board or council devotions become a model for the larger congregation, including committee meetings. The devotion first used at the board meeting is reintroduced at monthly team meetings. Those devotional experiences can then be taken home for people to reuse at home alone or with family and friends. Recycling the devotional life of a congregation's leadership from board meeting to other team meetings and on into individual homes fosters a congregational climate of Scripture reading, prayer, and other faith practices that anchors the congregation in Christ's love. Such a climate reflects a congregational administration that never loses sight of the reason for being: a community of faith whose life is born out of and daily renewed in the word of God.

Below is an example of a congregation that gives seasonal attention to the local food shelf. That concern and ministry is woven together with God's word in Scripture and other faith practices. Notice how fluidly the invitation to the larger congregation to bring food for the food shelf is interwoven with care and attention to their identity as followers of Jesus Christ. A council member in conversation with one of the congregation's pastors developed the devotional piece. The pastor then sent out the Four Key piece for use by various ministry teams and committees with a brief note by the pastor: "I invite you to use this special devotion for your February meeting and encourage support for the Food Shelf."

Bethany Committee and Ministry Team Devotions
FEBRUARY, 2010

Please use these Four Key devotions for your committee and ministry team meetings during the month of February. We are using this month to accomplish a major food drive effort for the Food Pantry. Please ask all members of your committee and ministry teams to bring nonperishable food items to your meeting as an act of service.

Devotions: Read John 6:1-14 "Feeding of the Five Thousand"
- What do you make of the difference in perspective between the disciples and Jesus in this scene? When asked about how the

people would get enough to eat the disciples said, "There is a boy here who has five barley loaves and two fish. But what are they among so many people?"

- On the other hand, Jesus took the loaves, and when he had given thanks, he distributed them to those who were seated; so also the fish, as much as they wanted. When they were satisfied, he told his disciples, "Gather up the fragments left over, so that nothing may be lost."
- How are the people fed?

Caring Conversations

- Talk about ways that Jesus has used and multiplied the gifts that that you have in order to bless others much more than you thought was possible.
- In this New Year, how do you think God will encourage you to continue to see new ways that your gifts will be multiplied in the future?
- How can making plans for your family's future, including its living expenses and giving, be opportunities to be blessed and to bless others with the abundance of God's gifts?

Service

- Bring your non-perishable food items together to be blessed and multiplied for the sake of the hungry in our community.

Rituals and Traditions

- Gather the food items together in the center of your table or meeting area.
- Light a candle and place it close to the food items so that the light reflects off the food offering that you have brought.
- Pray this prayer, or another one of your own choosing...

Lord, God of abundance, the light of your love shines on all that we have and all that we offer up to you. Let that light so shine through us that others may witness your love through these gifts. Bless this offering that it may be multiplied for the sake of those who are hungry in our community. We thank you for the witness of a young boy who trusted in your ability to move beyond limited imaginations. Send us out to go into life strengthened to follow Jesus Christ, the one who taught us to pray..."Our Father, who art in heaven..."

Administration that focuses on Christian faith practices as well as managing congregational services is the best way for a congregation to integrate faith and action. It guides pastoral supervision of staff; it shapes leadership teams as faith communities that seek to discern God's will instead of power groups that seek their own way. It expands the impact of Sunday worship to a way of life that is lived out in leadership groups and homes alike. It leads people to live lives that are authentically grounded in God's word, and available to the world God cares for, judges, and redeems; and it affirms that above all human volition, talking, praying and discerning God's will is the right way "to equip the saints for the work of ministry, for building up the body of Christ."

8

Church Facilities

This book provides all kinds of helpful and insightful recommendations for how you can develop a congregational mindset that embraces the Vibrant Faith Frame. As inspired and excited as you may find yourself, dear reader, and as eager as you may be to adopt new goals and implement new strategies for your congregation's future, before you rush into action there is one more important aspect of congregational life to consider: your church facility.

No matter how well you incorporate "home as church" into your ministry, your church building is very likely to remain a fundamental and critical tool. Typically, it's where the curious will come for the first time to experience your unique ministry and learn about your values, mission, and vision as a congregation. It's where your congregational family gathers regularly for worship, fellowship, and learning. For the larger community, your church facility is the physical and symbolic manifestation of who you are—and so it makes sense neither to ignore nor neglect its importance.

"Architecture Always Wins!"

In 1943, while exhorting Britain about the urgency of restoring the bombed-out Houses of Parliament, Winston Churchill famously declared, "First we shape our buildings, then they shape us." Congregations and parishes too often neglect or ignore this enduring truth when it comes to their own buildings. Worship styles, ministry objectives, and key programs all evolve and change, sometimes quickly, but it's common for our congregational buildings to remain unchanged for generations. Consequently, congregational staffs often discover that their shining new programs actually have to be pared back or adapted to accommodate unsympathetic facilities.

There's a corollary phenomenon in the world of church: art. Imagine a grace-centered Christian of today visiting the Byzantine church at the Daphni Monastery, outside Athens. Here the modern believer, raised on images of a loving, caring, compassionate and even smiling Jesus, encounters instead the eleventh-century version of our Lord! The frightening visage of Jesus in Daphni's mosaic is exceptionally stern, glowering angrily from above as the vengeful *Christ Pantocrator* – "Judge of all." While appropriate for the theology of its day, such a depiction of Jesus is be suitable in few congregations a millennium later. Can a sermon of grace and mercy truly be heard and accepted in Daphni's church today? The theology of the place has changed greatly, but the message of the mosaic endures nonetheless.

In truth, art and architecture both can work in opposition to our beliefs and values, sometimes without our noticing. As unthinkable as it may be to tolerate a mosaic, painting, or sculpture in the congregation's sanctuary that contradicts what we're trying to teach, congregations commonly tolerate outdated architectural design elements, insisting that ministry continue to conform to the values and practices for which the building was originally created.

A popular saying in the church design world reminds us that: "Whenever your ministry goals and your architecture are in conflict, architecture always wins." Architecture influences a congregation's ministry. It can facilitate, but it can also limit ministry.

" Architecture can also limit ministry. "

Assessing and appropriately responding to facilities challenges is critical if congregations are to achieve the effective and efficient ministries for which they strive. The whole process, from evaluation to taking action, can be a difficult task involving all kinds of resources, but the rewards are often nothing short of transformative for the congregation's ministry. Let's take a look at three examples of congregations that took on the challenge, and found themselves richly blessed by it.

Example One: Church of St. Peter

The Church of St. Peter strives to be a warm and gracious faith community. Hospitality, inclusiveness, and welcome are identified as core values, stated clearly and boldly in all parish publications, and displayed prominently on banners throughout the facility. "The work of cultivating relationships is *everything* here," Pastor Judy declared at our first meeting. But then she added, a bit wistfully, "At least, that's the way we *yearn* for it to be."

Each Sunday was an exercise in frustration for the leaders of the Church of St. Peter. Despite their persistent and sincere invitation to worshipers to stay after services and interact with each other over a cup of coffee, to build relationships through casual, caring conversations, each week all but a handful of folks would stream directly out of worship and toward their cars. You see, while the pastors and other leaders were offering words of warm invitation, the building was delivering an entirely different message.

The Church of St. Peter was designed several generations ago, and as was typical of that era, the main entrance to the building had only a small vestibule – essentially a hallway just wide enough for hanging coats and accommodating a few greeters. The after-worship activity of coffee fellowship, so critical to the congregation's ambitions, took place each week at the distant, opposite end of the rather large, single-level facility.

That the fellowship hall was so remote was only part of the problem, however. The main entrance to the 450-seat sanctuary was also the main exit. The conclusion of the worship service meant the funneling of hundreds of people into and through the small vestibule, creating a "cattle chute effect." Whomever the preacher was greeting could hardly help being self-consciousness about so many people still standing in line, waiting to leave the sanctuary. Rather than conveying a message of, "Stay a while, relax, get to know someone," the building instead was saying, "Get out! Leave! Move along! You're blocking the road!" The path of least resistance meant walking straight out the front door.

Today, as a result of a careful needs analysis, an excellent design, a compelling capital appeal, and well-managed construction, the Church of St. Peter has a bright, open and welcoming gathering space, complete with its own coffee preparation and serving area. Casual seating areas with comfortable sofas encourage relaxed and sustained conversations. A prominent office entrance, with receptionist, is immediately adjacent to the gathering space, convenient and obvious to those who are visiting for the first time. Opposite the offices, a new chapel with a garden view offers a more intimate space for rites and rituals, and small group or family gatherings.

> Space for listening, responding, caring, serving, and praying for others.

The Vibrant Faith Frame emphasizes that, "faith is formed by the power of the Holy Spirit through personal, trusted relationships." The Church of St. Peter now has a facility that's consistent with–rather than resistant to–that conviction. There is space for listening, responding, caring, serving, and praying for others. Hospitality is a valued Christian tradition, one that can now be lived more fluidly in the new facilities. That same tradition of Christian hospitality can be modeled in the congregation as well as modeled for the church in the home. The new space at St. Peter encourages living the Four Keys, and nurturing the Christian faith through AAA Christians – that is, people who are available to one another, not running out the door avoiding one another.

Example Two: Cliffside Church

Pastor David was heartbroken at the news that a member had just called to share. Yet another would-be first time visitor had been turned away at Cliffside Church–*his* church. Yet another person who wanted to meet Jesus was turned back at the parking lot, thanks to a building with "accessibility issues."

It wasn't the first time this had happened. Cliffside Church had been built 80 years earlier in this town of 5500 persons. At that time, it was typical to build the church with the main floor significantly above the grade of the surrounding land, partly to make possible more natural light in the basement fellowship hall, and partly to symbolize the significance of the worship space by literally elevating it. Once again, the popular design trends of a bygone day had serious repercussions.

Members and visitors with mobility impairments are nothing new, of course, but neither is the unfortunate message that many older church buildings send clearly to those so challenged. "We don't want you here," inaccessible congregational facilities declare. "Your diminished mobility diminishes your value to us. Stay away."

Pastor David was resolute. After the third report in a month that someone interested in Cliffside Church–someone who also happened to be confined to an electric-powered wheelchair –had simply given up at the base of the church's steep front steps, Pastor David was determined to find a solution.

"We're a small town church, in an aging community, and it's simply inexcusable that we have a funeral or wedding and people can't even get from the service to the fellowship hall... if they can even get into the building! That's certainly not the message that the congregation should be sending. We're wanting to grow as a congregation, for heaven's sake; we're trying to teach our kids to honor the elders among us – but meanwhile, our building is turning people away!"

" Our building is turning people away! "

In 1990, Congress passed the Americans With Disabilities Act, or ADA, as a means for remedying discrimination against persons for whom physical conditions – of body and building – create unequal access to public facilities, including congregations. It created very specific guidelines to ensure that all people have access to all public areas within a building. But for the people of Cliffside Church, their motivation in addressing accessibility issues wasn't merely to comply with the law. It was about faith active in love, a compassionate love that never excludes any of those for whom the gospel is intended. How could the people of Cliffside Church aspire to be "Authentic, *Available*, and Affirming" while blocking people with disabilities from coming in?

Unfortunately, overcoming accessibility issues–or any significant issues with an aging facility, for that matter–can be difficult and, as Cliffside Church discovered, prohibitively expensive. After a thorough analysis of their building and a projection of exactly what would be required to make it fully accessible, the congregation decided to relocate and build an entirely new facility–all on one level–that also solved their need for more worship and classroom space. Their new building has been a powerful symbol of hope and strength in a town where new construction projects of any kind are rare, and the initial surge in participation in worship and programs has continued in the years since construction was completed.

Example Three: Trinity Church

Trinity Church had developed and was working hard to implement big plans for youth and family ministry, plans that had been in the works for years. Their diligence and creativity were paying off, too; participants in children's programming had doubled. Youth programs were growing as well, and the word of about Trinity's unique vitality continued to spread throughout their small city.

"We had kids everywhere," Toni, the youth and family ministry coordinator, said with a proud smile. "But our biggest blessing was our biggest challenge, too!"

To put it mildly, Trinity Church's building was maxed out, especially at peak usage times. Creative scheduling could only accommodate so much of the growth, and the stress of multiple small groups, for example, all meeting simultaneously in the same room for discussion was wearing out staff, mentors, and students alike. "Literally every single space in the buildingn was being used," Toni recalled. "The offices, the hallways—even the kitchen had two small groups meeting in it."

Other ministries were sliding too. Trinity Church had recently completed a strategic planning process; the resulting report recommended that the congregation do much more to learn about and respond to the needs of the surrounding community. "Look outside your walls to discover your internal relevance," the report exhorted, and located as Trinity Church is just a couple of blocks from the city's center, the congregation was ready and eager to embrace a new mission of service and outreach. A fast-tracked mission planning effort resulted in strategies that would surely rival the success of their youth program—until those plans needed to be put on hold due to the lack of meeting, storage, meal serving, and clinic space in Trinity's current facility.

"Our building isn't even all that old," Toni reflected. "But the leaders at the time of its construction never anticipated that we'd be where we are today, with so much going on and so many people involved. Right now the building is preventing us from being and doing everything God's calling us to be and do."

A popular saying in church circles is that "if you're not growing, you're losing momentum." Failing to respond to a need for more space doesn't only prevent expansion of ministry and growth in participation; it can also frustrate and potentially alienate current participants in existing programs. Church designers serve their clients best when they anticipate future growth and master plans include opportunities for eventual expansion.

In the case of Trinity Church, an investigation of the city's building code and restrictions revealed that the congregation was already as large–in fact, slightly larger–than was permitted in a residential area. An expansion of the building also would have triggered the need for additional off-street parking; adjacent homes would need to be purchased, and the alley that separated the congregation from those properties would have to be vacated. More restrooms were needed, and the existing restrooms had to be improved to meet ADA standards. Modern fire protection, including a monitored sprinkler system, would have to be installed to bring the facility "up to code."

Trinity Church found itself at what looked like a dead end–until someone suggested to Toni that the recently closed grocery store a block away would make a "pretty darn cool youth facility." In that moment, the congregation found itself faced with an extraordinary opportunity, thanks to a property that had abundant parking, a highly visible location, complete accessibility (even a loading dock!), and ample room not just for youth, but for all kinds of ministry ambitions. Having identified and quantified its space needs ahead of time, the congregation's leaders found the concept an easy sell to the larger congregation, and today the former grocery store is a center of ministry activity, where the youngest and oldest members alike gather for learning, fellowship, and service in a unique, cross+generational space. Even more, the building has become the prominent and primary interface between the larger community and the congregation's thriving outreach programs.

"This space has helped transform how we think of ourselves as the body of Christ," Toni exclaimed with genuine excitement. "Our dreams about becoming a missional church suddenly sprouted legs and walked right out into the real world. Today, we feel we're truly making a difference!"

> This space has helped transform how we think of ourselves as the body of Christ.

What about MY Congregation?

As these three examples demonstrate, a congregation's building has the potential to be a wonderful asset and tool for facilitating the Vibrant Faith Frame, just as it can be a powerful adversary working against you in all kinds of ways. As you consider the future to which God may be calling your congregation's ministry, does your building advance your cause, or obstruct it? Truly, the critical importance of this question should compel you to take a close, discerning look at your facility.

When we've been working in the same place for a long time, it's nearly impossible to see things objectively. In such cases it can be extremely helpful to invite an "outsider"—a friend from another congregation, for example, someone who is familiar with the value and importance of efficient, helpful church building design, but who hasn't seen your facility before—to come and do a careful and thoughtful analysis. (There are professional church building consultants and designers who can also assist you in this, sometimes at no cost.) You may be surprised at what such a consultant can see through a set of "new eyes."

To aid you in your own informal facility assessment, here are some questions for you (or a team of interested people) to consider:

- In what kind of condition is the congregation's sign? The parking lot? Are there cracks and weeds? Is there adequate striping?
- How welcoming and inviting are the landscaping features of the congregation's property?
- How easy is the main entrance to find? Are there curbs, steps, or other barriers that limit access to the building?
- Once inside, is it clear and obvious where visitors would find the worship center? Offices? Restrooms? Coat racks? Someone to greet and welcome visitors, and answer their questions?
- How does the gathering space/narthex "feel"? Is it warm and welcoming? Large enough (it should be at least 40-45% of the total square footage of the sanctuary)? Well-lighted? Are there casual seating areas suitable for caring conversations, and making new acquaintances? Is there a hospitality area nearby for serving refreshments and sharing ministry information?

- What is the quality of sound and light in the worship space? Can people everywhere see what's going on? Is there digital projection? An assisted listening system? Space among your seating for wheelchairs?
- Is there sufficient seating? The "80% full rule" deserves to be taken seriously: if 80% or more of your seats are occupied, additional people arriving are likely to perceive that there's no room left for them. It may be time to add another service, add seating, or expand or replace your worship space!
- Is your facility, including elevators and restrooms, fully ADA compliant? (The "1991 ADA Standards for Accessible Design" can be downloaded free from the U.S. Department of Justice at *www.ada.gov/stdspdf.htm.*)
- Do your restrooms have sufficient numbers of fixtures? Are there appropriately sized fixtures for small children? Diaper changing stations in appropriate locations (including for dads)?
- Do you have an attractive, welcoming, and safe nursery space, located near the worship center? Does it have a direct egress to the exterior of the building, for fire safety? A secure check-in counter? A hand sink? Appropriate floor and wall surfaces? Approved cribs?
- Do you have a sufficient number of classrooms, each sized appropriately for the number of occupants you currently have—and adequate to accommodate growth?
- Does your facility have a fire protection (sprinkler) system? Is it monitored?
- Are your offices conveniently located, and identified with adequate signage?
- Are individual offices well lighted, kept neat and uncluttered? Do visitors feel comfortable? Is there adequate room for a small meeting table and chairs?
- Do office and classroom doors have clear, unobstructed sidelights or other windows for security and safety?

- Is your fellowship hall an appropriate size for your needs? What's the condition of the carpet or other flooring? What's the quality of the lighting and sound system?
- Is the kitchen code-compliant for how you use it? (Many congregational kitchens do not need to have commercial-use finishes!)
- Are your locksets and door hardware ADA compliant? (If you still have round doorknobs, you're not up to code.)
- Do you have a large, multi-purpose space for activity by people of all ages?
- Do you readily make your facility available for use by community organizations? Do you have clear and printed, readily available policies about who can use the facilities, and under what circumstances? Is it clear who can use them with or without a usage fee, and why? Do the usage policies themselves feel welcome and inviting, or exclusive and exclusionary? Do you advertise that your facilities are available to others? How?
- Are the various rooms—including staff office—inviting for caring conversation, reflection, and prayer? Is the lighting harsh or soft? Are there plants, statues, natural lighting, and attractive wall hangings that convey God's gift of life, grace, peace, and creativity?
- Do the building spaces show a connection to the surrounding community? To the care of God's creation? To the presence of various people and cultures around the globe?
- Review your mission and vision statements and assess if the building space complements or resists the language. Do the rooms suggest to people, "Come as you are, stay and grow"–or some other message?

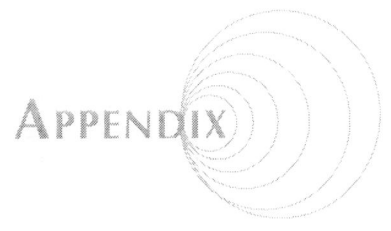

Appendix

6 SIX LOCATIONS of ministry
- Children and youth
- Homes
- Congregations
- Community
- Culture
- Creation

5 FIVE PRINCIPLES of a vibrant church
- Faith is formed by the power of the Holy Spirit through personal trusted relationships—often in our own homes.
- The church is a living partnership between the ministry of the congregation and ministry of the home.
- Where Christ is present in faith, the home is church, too.
- Faith is caught more than it is taught.
- If we want Christian children and youth, we need Christian adults.

4 FOUR KEYS for practicing faith
- Caring Conversations
- Devotions
- Service
- Rituals and Traditions

3 THREE CHARACTERISTICS of Christian disciples
- Authentic
- Available
- Affirming

FOR THOSE WHO ATTENDED A BAPTISM OR DEDICATION

In the days following the baptism or dedication of a friend or family member, consider the following Four Key faith practices:

Caring Conversation

Discuss how you can support the recently baptized or dedicated person(s). How can you support them and their family and friends on their journey of faith?

Tell the story of your baptism or dedication. What do you remember? What have you been told about it? Who was present with you?

Baptisms and dedications call upon the work and will of God to raise people of Christian faith. What does it mean to you that faith itself is a gift of God?

Devotions

- Read the story of the baptisms of the Philippian jailor and his household (Acts 16:25-34).
- Read the story of Jesus' naming and being presented in the temple by his parents (Luke 2:21-35).
- Read Isaiah 43:1-7.

Pray this prayer

Dear God, you call us by name and claim us as your sons and daughters. Come Holy Spirit, renew us in faith and in good courage as your disciples that we may bring your message of grace, mercy, healing, and salvation to all. In the name of Jesus Christ. Amen.

Service

- Jesus says that to follow him is to be a servant (see Mark 10:41–45). How do you think God has gifted you to serve others?
- Encourage the newly baptized and the families of children recently dedicated or baptized in living out the faith through Christian worship and fellowship.
- As a follower of Jesus, do a simple act of service for someone you do not know well.

Rituals and Traditions

Dip your hand into a bowl of water and consider how this vital element in creation is used as a sign of baptism. You may want to make the sign of the cross on your forehead or over your chest.

Prior to attending a worship service, pray for those who have been entrusted with the leadership of the worship service. Pray that the Spirit of Christ will be their source of wisdom, faithfulness, and witness.

Four Key Faith Practices for Your Honeymoon

As you begin your married life together, may these foundational faith practices enrich your honeymoon and serve as a lifelong pattern for your love for each other.

Caring Conversations
- What nice surprise did you experience on your wedding day?
- What was the funniest thing that happened on your wedding day?
- What words of wisdom or encouragement meant the most to you?

Devotions
Read Colossians 3:12-14 aloud to each other on each day of your honeymoon.

> *"As God's chosen ones, holy and beloved, clothe yourselves with compassion, kindness, humility, meekness, and patience. Bear with one another and, if anyone has a complaint against another, forgive each other; just as the Lord has forgiven you, so you also must forgive. Above all, clothe yourselves with love, which binds everything together in perfect harmony."*

Say this or another prayer:

> *Dear God, we give thanks to you for our love for each other. May our home be holy ground to each other and to all who enter the place where we dwell. Help us together to care for all you have given us and to await the marriage feast that has no end. In the name of Christ. Amen.*

Service

- As you enjoy your honeymoon, consider ways to care for others along your path, people who are fellow travelers, waiters and waitresses, hotel staff, and others.
- Make sure your happiness on your honeymoon includes the happiness of your spouse.
- When you return home, consider supporting with your service and/or money an organization that serves the needs of others.

Rituals and Traditions

When you retire for the night or when you arise in the morning bless each other with the words, "Let the word of Christ dwell in you richly" (Colossians 3:16).

Say this or another table grace before each meal:

Dear God, we thank you for this food, a sign of your constant love for us. Help us to be servants of your love to others. In the name of Jesus Christ. Amen.

Bulletin Insert for Funeral/ Memorial Service

We at *[name of congregation]* offer you these faith practices to take with you and use as you continue to grieve with the comfort and assurance offered through the Christian faith and Scriptures.

Caring Conversations

Use one or more of these conversation starters with family or friends.

- What did you learn about *[name]* that you did not know much about before the funeral/memorial service?
- What was it about *[name's]* life and faith that impressed you most?
- How would you like to keep *[name's]* life and memory as an important part of your own faith journey?

Devotions

A common funeral text is Psalm 23. It begins, "The Lord is my shepherd, I shall not want." Use that opening verse as a prayer and say it to yourself repeatedly. Reflect upon the kind of God that we have who is referred to as "my shepherd" and through whom we have no need of want.

Read one or more of the following Scripture texts: John 11:21–27; John 14:1-6; Romans 8:31-35, 37-39; 1 Corinthians 15:12-26; Revelation 21:2-7. Take time after the readings for silence and then conclude by praying the Lord's Prayer.

Pray the Lord's Prayer:

Our Father, who art in heaven, hallowed by thy name, thy kingdom come, thy will be done, on earth as it is in heaven. Give us this day our daily bread; and forgive us our trespasses, as we forgive those who trespass against us; and lead us not into temptation, but deliver us from evil. For thine is the kingdom, and the power, and the glory, forever and ever. Amen.

Service

- How did *[name's]* service of others influence how you want to care for people and God's creation?
- What memorial contribution(s) would best reflect your thanksgiving for *[name]*?
- What act of service would reflect your thanksgiving for *[name's]* life?

Rituals and Traditions

Light a candle at mealtime in memory of [name] and say this grace:

Dear God, we receive this food with thankful hearts, and we remember [name] with thanksgiving as you gave her/him to us to know and to love. Comfort our grief with your promise of life eternal through Christ our Lord. Amen.

Plant a tree or other plant in memory of *[name]*.

As you continue to grieve the death of *[name]* and reflect on the brevity of life, commit to regular Scripture reading and prayer.

ENDNOTES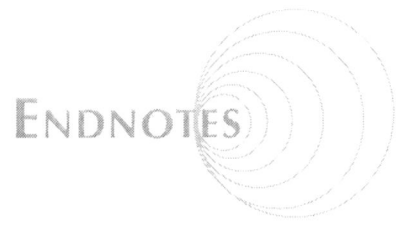

Chapter 1

1. See article by Alan Hirsch, "Defining Missional," at http://www. christianitytoday.com/le/2008/fall/17.20.html.

2. As quoted by John W. Matthews in *Anxious Souls Will Ask . . . The Christ-Centered Spirituality of Dietrich Bonhoeffer* (Grand Rapids: Eerdmans Publishing Company, 2005), 21.

3. Vibrant Faith Ministries has worked with congregations that assumed the larger community knew they were an active, local congregation, only to be surprised by the numbers of people who had no idea who or where the congregation was

4. Henri J.M. Nouwen, *Reaching Out: The Three Movements of the Spiritual Life* (Garden City: Doubleday & Company, Inc., 1975), 47.

5. Diana Butler Bass, *Christianity for the Rest of Us* (New York: HarperOne, 2006), 83-4.

6. See *From the Great Omission to Vibrant Faith: The Role of the Home in Renewing the Church* (Minneapolis: Vibrant Faith Publishing, 2009), chapters 1 and 3.

7. A resource available from Vibrant Faith Publishing (www.vibrant-faith.org) to help stimulate conversation between adults and young people on issues surrounding their beliefs and values. It is now available as a smart phone app to further draw attention to the importance of immediate conversation about the Christian faith, especially for younger generations ready and willing to try this platform for conversations about spiritual matters.

8. Nilsen, *For Everything a Season: 75 Blessings for Daily Life* (Minneapolis: Vibrant Faith Publishing, 1999).

Chapter 2

1. See *From the Great Omission to Vibrant Faith: the Role of the Home in Renewing the Church*, chapters 1 and 3, by David W. Anderson (Vibrant Faith Publishing, 2009).

2. See significant pieces of this data summarized at www.vibrantfaith.org/documents/ResearchPP-logo10.26.09.pdf

3. Kristen Venne, *The Family as the Center of Faith Formation: A Study of the Connection between Home and Congregation in the Faith Lives of Families in Congregations Implementing the Child In Our Hands Initiative*, thesis submitted to the faculty of Luther Seminary, St. Paul, MN, 2007, 127.

4. *Growing Up Religious*, xxxvii.

5. Venne, 112.

6. Venne, 112.

7. To learn more about FaithChests® as an important part of the faith journey in homes and congregations, contact Vibrant Faith Ministries at www.vibrantfaith.org.

8. Christian Smith with Patricia Snell, *Souls in Transition: The Religious & Spiritual Lives of Emerging Adults* (New York: Oxford University Press, 2009), 216.

Chapter 3

1. Venne, p. 127.

2. For an exegesis of this text as it relates to the Four Keys, see *Frogs without Legs Can't Hear: Nurturing Disciples in Home and Congregation* (Minneapolis: Augsburg Fortress, 2003), 104-5.

3. During Abraham Lincoln's second inaugural address, recently freed slaves began to chant, "Praise the Lord" after each of his sentences. What an appropriate response to such a dramatic moment in the history of the United States of America. What an appropriate and faithful response to a dramatic moment in the lives of Christians.

4. *Taking Faith Home* is written by Pastor Greg Priebbenow and is available at VFM.

5. This research technique is explored in depth in *From the Great Omission to Vibrant Faith: The Role of the Home in Renewing the Church* (Bloomington: Vibrant Faith Publishing, 2009), 132-4.

6. Dawn Rundman, *Splash* (Minneapolis: Augsburg Fortress, ongoing).

7. See "Three Decades of Research on Faith Formation," www.vibrantfaith.org/documents/ResearchPP-logo10.26.09.pdf

8. See www.faithfactors.com for a complete list of factors that influence the faith life and church loyalty of young people.

9. The next book in this series, *Vibrant Faith in the Home*, will give ample testimony to that arena of the life of the church.

Chapter 4

1. For the past twenty-five years, the staff of the former TYFI and now VFM has championed the role of the home in the lives of faith formation of youth. That is why the Great Omission (the neglect of the role of the home) was addressed in the first book of this Vibrant Faith: Home and Congregation Series. For more details on the research, see Three Decades of Research on Faith Formation at www.vibrantfaith.org/documents/ResearchPP-logo10.26.09.pdf

2. Roland Martinson, Wes Black, and John Roberto, *The Spirit and Culture of Youth Ministry: Leading Congregations toward Exemplary Youth Ministry* (St. Paul: EYM Publishing, 2010), 24.

3. See summary of three decades of research at www.vibrantfaith.org.

4. For this and more information, see the website www.faithfactors.com.

5. See David W. Anderson, *From the Great Omission to Vibrant Faith: the Role of the Home in Renewing the Church* (Vibrant Faith Publishing, 2009).

6. See "From Christian Education to Faith Formation" for an exploration of how mission trips can be Vibrant Faith Frame experiences.

7. To learn more about Peer Ministry, check out www.peerministry.org.

8. Quoted from *Coming of Age: Exploring the Identity and Spirituality of Younger Men* by David W. Anderson, Paul G. Hill, and Roland D. Martinson (Minneapolis: Augsburg Fortress, 2006), 81.

9. Mindy Bak, *Together in Faith* (Vibrant Faith Publishing, second edition, 2011).

Chapter 5

1. The resource used by the congregation is *Taking Faith Home*, a bulletin insert that offers examples of each of the Four Keys based on the lectionary texts recommended for each Sunday of the church year. Available from VFM at www.vibrantfaith.org.

2. See www.nytimes.com/2009/08/09/science/earth/09climate.html for more details.

3. See www.bread.org/hunger/global for more details.

4. See water.org/learn-about-the-water-crisis/facts for more details.

5. See www.webofcreation.org/ for more information on a faith-based and congregational focus on creation care.

6. Learn about Strength Finders at www.strengthsfinder.com/home.aspx and about Dependable Strengths at www.dependablestrengths.org/.

Chapter 6

1. See *The Handbook of Spiritual Development in Childhood and Adolescence*, ed. Eugene C. Roehlkepartain, Pamela Ebstyne King, Linda Wagener, and Peter L. Benson (Thousand Oaks: Sage Publications, 2006) and *Nurturing Child and Adolescent Spirituality: Perspectives from the World's Religious Traditions*, ed. Karen Marie Yust, Aostre N. Johnson, Sandy Eisenberg Sasso, and Eugene C. Roehlkepartain (Lanham: Rowman & Littlefield Publishers, Inc., 2006).

2. Check out the results of this mentoring program at http://cfsd.chipfalls.k12.wi.us/cvMentors.cfm.

Chapter 7

1. See John Kotter's list of eight reasons why change efforts fail and how to address it: http://kotterinternational.com/KotterPrinciples/ChangeSteps.aspx?gclid=CNC4yrOKo6UCFRBNgwoduzUnGg

2. The Congregational Leaders Series of Augsburg Fortress has a wealth of such useful, hands-on examples and processes, as does The Alban Institute and the Lewis Center for Church Leadership.

ACKNOWLEDGMENTS

This book's contribution to the life of the church does not result from only one person's insights or authorship. *Vibrant Faith in the Congregation* is the result of support, insights, critique, and concrete examples from many sources. First of all, the positive energy and commitment to the work of the church is evident in the Vibrant Faith Ministry team. Without them, there would be no book or Vibrant Faith Home and Congregation in Partnership Series. Thank you Ginger and Larry Anderson, Julie Diedrich, Jim LaDoux, Patty Matthews, John Roberto, and Sue Turgeon. A special thanks to Paul Hill, executive director and the person who made sure this book became a reality. The same accolades can be given to the VFM board of directors, lead by Dr. Nancy Going, whose vision and commitment to VFM is unwavering.

Along the way of conceiving and writing this book, a whole host of people contributed conversations, ideas, and examples that eventually made their way into *Vibrant Faith in the Congregation*. Thanks to: Tonia Andersen, Karen Birkedal, Paula Davis, Carol DeJardin, Peter Eckermann, Jeff Elmquist, Andrea Fieldhouse, Tim Glenham, Paul Hanson, Fred Harms, Karen Hofstad, Kristin Hildebrand, Dave Keck, Darrell Kyle, Ken Langsdorf, Shannyn Magee, Tom Morgan, John Mouritsen, Paul Nelson, Arja Owens, Mike Pancoast, Greg Priebbenow, Jeff Rohr, Wade Rouser, Roger Skatrud, Russ Sorensen, Chip Stokes, Carol Tomer,

Kristen Venne, Dan Warnes, Gary Weant, Susan Weaver, Brigette Weier, Connie Weiss, Tammy Jones West, Joanne Wiedman, and Greg Williams. Without their passion for the church and commitment to VFM, this book would not have materialized.

I offer a special word of thanks to three readers of the final manuscript, servants of the church who are committed to the life and work of the church. Dick Bruesehoff, Greg Kaufmann, and Bill Tesch provided their unique and field-tested perspectives to the manuscript. They all read the manuscript with an eye to the need for the church to reach out to the surrounding community and larger world. Alongside their recommendations resides the very solid work of the book's project director, Bill Huff and Huff Publishing and the very fine editing of Ulrike (Uli) Guthrie. It is a better book because of their combined efforts in this writing project.

The reader will note that the final chapter, "Church Facilities," is written by Richard Wehrs. I want to thank Dick, a pastor, associate at VFM, and project development consultant specializing in church facilities. His dedication to the Vibrant Faith Frame over the years has influenced his personal and professional life in a way that has been a true gift to the work of VFM. The enthusiasm and dedication he brings to the final chapter offer the reader a fresh perspective that adds to the overall benefit of the book. For that we at VFM are all thankful.

Finally, with deep sadness this book is published in memory of Jim Mullen. Vibrant Faith Ministries lost Jim, a dear member of our team, on January 20, 2011. After a five-year struggle with cancer, operations manager Jim Mullen passed away at the age of 53. Jim was a devoted employee of VFM for seven years. He managed all of VFM's shipping, accounting, inventory, and organizational operations. Many will remember Jim as the voice of VFM as he was usually the one who answered the phone. Jim staunchly believed in the mission of VFM and brought great passion to his work. And long after many would have resigned themselves to their fate, Jim continued to work until he simply could not go on any longer. "He was the toughest guy I've ever known," said Dr. Paul Hill. "He never complained about his very painful illness and treatments. He never said, 'Why me?' His faith took the form of serving the church through VFM." We have lost a dear friend, co-worker, and colleague, and many within and beyond the VFM family will miss him. We commend Jim to Jesus Christ, confident that he rests in the loving arms of his Savior. Jim is survived by his wife Sandy, daughter Kari, and many other family and friends.

Vibrant Faith in the Home
Coming in 2012

Vibrant Faith in the Home is the final installment of the three-part Vibrant Faith: Home and Congregation series. *Vibrant Faith in the Home* gives individuals, couples, and larger families/households practical, relatable suggestions on how to apply the Vibrant Faith Frame to the home setting. In addition to being filled with inspirational stories about people who live the Four Keys on a daily basis, this book also reveals how particular milestones in people's lives connect the faith life of their homes with the larger world around them.

From the Great Omission to Vibrant Faith: The Role of the Home in Renewing the Church

First book in the three-part
Vibrant Faith: Home and Congregation Series
by Dr. David Anderson (2009)

Parents play the most important role in the vibrant faith formation of their children. Yet, many congregations are failing to equip parents and other caring adults with the tools they need to nurture and grow the faith of the young people in their churches. The good news is that it is not too late to fix this problem. The author, Dr. David Anderson, traces how this "Great Omission" has happened and what we can do to challenge our youth to live lives of faith and service. This is a wonderful resource for congregational leaders, parents, grandparents, and adults who seek a vibrant faith in Jesus Christ for themselves and their children.

Other books by David Anderson

Frogs without Legs Can't Hear
Nurturing Disciples in Home and Congregation
David W. Anderson and Paul G. Hill

Comparing church to a frog?

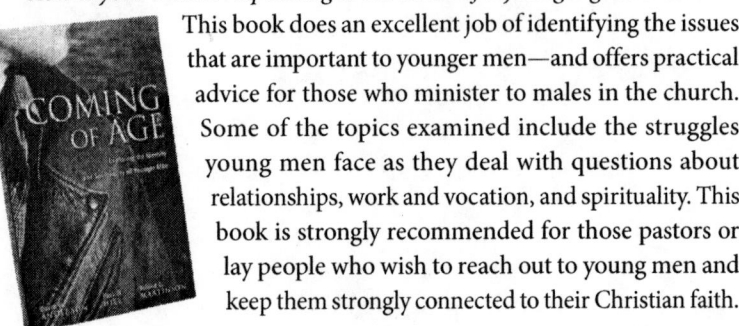

It might seem like a crazy analogy—but beyond the comparison is a very readable book based on Scripture, research, and experience that creates a cultural shift in how faith formation is typically practiced. The theory is that it takes a whole church "frog" (the head is leadership, the torso is the congregation, and the legs are the home) to build a true Christian community and nurture faith in young people. The result is a more effective ministry that includes a stronger congregation-home partnership.

Coming of Age
Exploring the Spirituality and Identity of Younger Men
David W. Anderson, Paul G. Hill, and Roland D. Martinson

How is your church responding to the needs of a younger generation?

This book does an excellent job of identifying the issues that are important to younger men—and offers practical advice for those who minister to males in the church. Some of the topics examined include the struggles young men face as they deal with questions about relationships, work and vocation, and spirituality. This book is strongly recommended for those pastors or lay people who wish to reach out to young men and keep them strongly connected to their Christian faith.

**To order books and resources from Vibrant Faith Ministries,
go to www.vibrantfaith.org or call 877-239-2492.**